# LIVING PEACEFULLY

Selection and introduction by Zachary Seager

M

MACMILLAN COLLECTOR'S LIBRARY

This collection first published 2025 by Macmillan Collector's Library
an imprint of Pan Macmillan
The Smithson, 6 Briset Street, London EC1M 5NR
*EU representative:* Macmillan Publishers Ireland Ltd,
1st Floor, The Liffey Trust Centre, 117–126 Sheriff Street Upper,
Dublin 1, D01 YC43
Associated companies throughout the world
www.panmacmillan.com

ISBN 978-1-0350-4564-8

Introduction copyright © Zachary Seager 2025
Selection and arrangement copyright © Macmillan Publishers International Ltd. 2025

The Permissions Acknowledgements on p. 211 constitute
an extension of this copyright page.

1 3 5 7 9 8 6 4 2

A CIP catalogue record for this book is available from the British Library.

Typeset in Platin by Jouve (UK), Milton Keynes
Printed and bound in China by Imago

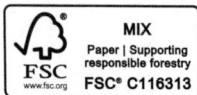

MIX
Paper | Supporting
responsible forestry
FSC
www.fsc.org
FSC® C116313

Visit **www.panmacmillan.com** to read more
about all our books and to buy them.

# Contents

PEACE IN THE WORLD

# Introduction

Peace – inner, outer, interpersonal, international –
is universally recognized as a Good Thing, one
of life's chief goals and, in many ways, the
noblest. The idea of peace unites us all. How
it might be achieved causes confusion, division
and, in many cases, war.

We all desire peace but we erect barriers to it
everywhere. Entire economies are built on distraction and disturbance, on the destruction of
our environment and the disruption of our minds.
How then can we make space for the pursuit of
tranquility? We design our lives around product-
ivity and efficiency – the fundamental values of
technology, of machines. Encouraged constantly
to do more, to strive more, to achieve more, how
can we justify our need for peace in the first
place? At the same time, we seem perpetually on

the verge of global conflict. How can we keep faith in a peaceful future?

These questions might seem new and uniquely modern. But they have exercised the minds of some of history's most influential thinkers. This anthology gathers classic works by major authors alongside lesser-known writers, all of whom have considered peace in its various forms – peace of mind, peace in the world and the peace we can find or make around ourselves every day.

Some authors consider the question of what to do with our peaceful hours, the idle instants extolled by the humorist Jerome K. Jerome and analyzed with piercing irony by the novelist Rose Macaulay. Japanese scholar and critic Okakura Kakuzō describes the path to peace through ritual and tradition. And Agnes Repplier, a prolific and acclaimed essayist, discusses the many forms of leisure practised by past peoples, bringing us closer to bygone eras and offering new ideas for the future. She has a radical vision of idle hours: for Repplier, leisure is not only pleasurable for individuals but necessary for society.

Each of these authors offers a different path to peace and a different view of peaceful hours, from the intricacies of the Japanese tea ceremony to spending time in bed (Macaulay's essay 'Bed' is usefully divided into two parts: 'getting into it' and 'not getting out of it'). Meanwhile, the revered Scottish writer Robert Louis Stevenson helps us justify our pursuit of leisure: he vigorously defends loafers, layabouts and idlers of all sorts, all while seeing in rest and relaxation an integral part of life.

One can, however, quietly pour tea with an unquiet mind. Anxious waves can pitch, toss and sway us even as we seek sleep. And in the most tranquil places – a verdant Swiss valley, say, with breathtaking mountain views – stress and strife can seize us. In other words, there can be a tense gap between a supposedly peaceful activity and the real calm we find there. But this distance depends not on the mountains or the valley but on ourselves – on our peace of mind.

What is peace of mind and how exactly can we attain it? Trailblazing novelist D. H. Lawrence offers an elegant solution to the problem: insouciance. Poet and essayist Hilaire Belloc gives us good reason to change our attitudes towards rest and leisure. And Roman statesman and philosopher Seneca proposes an entire ethical system dedicated to achieving inner peace.

As a thinker in the Stoic tradition, Seneca

argues that we have real power over our own thoughts and emotions. By instructing us to focus on what we can and can't control, he shows that peace of mind is not only within our grasp but that, in important ways, it can only come from within us and us alone. In this way, Seneca – like Lawrence, Stevenson, Macaulay and many others – tells us that though peace on earth seems unattainable, inner peace is within our reach.

These writers all describe different ways of cultivating our gardens, as Voltaire put it in his classic tale *Candide*. In other words, they focus on what we as individuals can influence and develop about ourselves and our environment. It would be foolish, they imply, to wish to solve other people's problems or to reflect on something so absurd as, for instance, world peace.

In the final section of this anthology, major writers and thinkers turn their thoughts to just such an absurd question. James Boswell – one of the greatest biographers in the English language – considers the brute stupidity of war. Virginia Woolf, present in London during the Blitz, finds the presence of mind to think not of bombs but of peace. And in his acceptance speech for the Nobel Peace Prize, Martin Luther

King Jr discusses discrimination, inequality and injustice in painful terms. But he never loses sight of his ultimate ambition: peace.

This anthology shows that just as there are different kinds of peace, there are many ways to find it. Each text offers not only deep thought and entertainment but also a method and a course of action, a path to living peacefully.

# Peace
# of Mind

D. H. LAWRENCE

# Insouciance

My balcony is on the east side of the hotel, and my neighbours on the right are a Frenchman, white-haired, and his white-haired wife; my neighbours on the left are two little white-haired English ladies. And we are all mortally shy of one another.

When I peep out of my room in the morning and see the matronly French lady in a purple silk wrapper, standing like the captain on the bridge surveying the morning, I pop in again before she can see me. And whenever I emerge during the day, I am aware of the two little white-haired ladies popping back like two white rabbits, so that literally I only see the whisk of their skirt-hems.

This afternoon being hot and thundery, I woke up suddenly and went out on the balcony barefoot. There I sat serenely contemplating the world, and ignoring the two bundles of feet

3

of the two little ladies which protruded from their open doorways, upon the end of the two *chaises longues*. A hot, still afternoon! the lake shining rather glassy away below, the mountains rather sulky, the greenness very green, all a little silent and lurid, and two mowers mowing with scythes, downhill just near: *slush! slush!* sound the scythe-strokes.

The two little ladies become aware of my presence. I become aware of a certain agitation in the two bundles of feet wrapped in two discreet steamer rugs and protruding on the end of two *chaises longues* from the pair of doorways upon the balcony next me. One bundle of feet suddenly disappears; so does the other. Silence!

Then lo! with odd sliding suddenness a little white-haired lady in grey silk, with round blue eyes, emerges and looks straight at me, and remarks that it is pleasant now. A little cooler, say I, with false amiability. She quite agrees, and we speak of the men mowing; how plainly one hears the long breaths of the scythes!

By now we are *tête-à-tête*. We speak of cherries, strawberries, and the promise of the vine crop. This somehow leads to Italy, and to Signor Mussolini. Before I know where I am, the little white-haired lady has swept me off my balcony, away from the glassy lake, the veiled mountains, the two men mowing, and the cherry trees, away into the troubled ether of international politics.

I am not allowed to sit like a dandelion on my own stem. The little lady in a breath blows me abroad. And I was so pleasantly musing over the two men mowing: the young one, with long legs in bright blue cotton trousers, and with bare black head, swinging so lightly downhill, and the other, in black trousers, rather stout in front, and wearing a new straw hat of the boater variety, coming rather stiffly after, crunching the end of his stroke with a certain violent effort.

I was watching the curiously different motions of the two men, the young thin one in bright blue trousers, the elderly fat one in shabby black trousers that stick out in front, the different amount of effort in their mowing, the lack of grace in the elderly one, his jerky advance, the unpleasant effect of the new "boater" on his head—and I tried to interest the little lady.

But it meant nothing to her. The mowers, the mountains, the cherry trees, the lake, all the things that were *actually* there, she didn't care about. They even seemed to scare her off the balcony. But she held her ground, and instead of herself being scared away, she snatched me up like some ogress, and swept me off into the empty desert spaces of right and wrong, politics, Fascism and the rest.

The worst ogress couldn't have treated me more villainously. I don't care about right and wrong, politics, Fascism, abstract liberty or anything else of the sort. I want to look at the mowers, and wonder why fatness, elderliness and black trousers should inevitably wear a new straw hat of the boater variety, move in stiff jerks, shove the end of the scythe-stroke with a certain violence, and win my hearty disapproval, as contrasted with young long thinness, bright blue cotton trousers, a bare black head, and a pretty lifting movement at the end of the scythe-stroke.

Why do modern people almost invariably ignore the things that are actually present to them? Why, having come out from England to find mountains, lakes, scythe-mowers and cherry trees, does the little blue-eyed lady resolutely close her blue eyes to them all, now she's got them, and gaze away to Signor Mussolini, whom she hasn't got, and to Fascism, which is invisible anyhow? Why isn't she content to be where she is? Why can't she be happy with what she's got? Why must she *care*?

I see now why her round blue eyes are so

round, so noticeably round. It is because she "cares." She is haunted by that mysterious bugbear of "caring." For everything on earth that doesn't concern her she "cares." She cares terribly because far-off, invisible, hypothetical Italians wear black shirts, but she doesn't care a rap that one elderly mower whose stroke she can hear, wears black trousers instead of bright blue cotton ones. Now if she would descend from the balcony and climb the grassy slope and say to the fat mower: *Cher monsieur, pourquoi portez-vous les pantalons noirs?* Why, oh, why do you wear black trousers?"—then I should say: What an on-the-spot little lady!—But since she only torments me with international politics, I can only remark: What a tiresome off-the-spot old woman!

They care! They simply are eaten up with caring. They are so busy caring about Fascism or Leagues of Nations or whether France is right or whether Marriage is threatened, that they never know where they are. They certainly never live on the spot where they are. They inhabit abstract space, the desert void of politics, principles, right and wrong, and so forth. They are doomed to be abstract. Talking to them is like trying to have a human relationship with the letter $x$ in algebra.

There simply is a deadly breach between actual

living and this abstract caring. What is actual living? It is a question mostly of direct contact. There was a direct sensuous contact between me, the lake, mountains, cherry trees, mowers, and a certain invisible but noisy chaffinch in a clipped lime tree. All this was cut off by the fatal shears of that abstract word Fascism, and the little old lady next door was the Atropos who cut the thread of my actual life this afternoon. She beheaded me, and flung my head into abstract space. Then we are supposed to love our neighbours!

When it comes to living, we live through our instincts and our intuitions. Instinct makes me run from little over-earnest ladies; instinct makes me sniff the lime blossom and reach for the darkest cherry. But it is intuition which makes me feel the uncanny glassiness of the lake this afternoon, the sulkiness of the mountains, the vividness of near green in thunder-sun, the young man in bright blue trousers lightly tossing the grass from the scythe, the elderly man in a boater stiffly shoving his scythe-strokes, both of them sweating in the silence of the intense light.

HILAIRE BELLOC

# On Rest

Rest is not the conclusion of labour but the re-creation of power. It seems a reward because it fulfils a need: but that need being filled, Rest is but an extinction and a nothingness. So we do not pray for Rest; but (in a just religion) we pray after this life for refreshment, light and peace—not for Rest.

Rest is only for a little while, as also is labour only for a little while: each demanding the other as a supplement; yet is Rest in some intervals a necessary ground for seed, and without Rest to protect the sprouting of the seed no good thing ever grew.

Of many follies in a Commonwealth concerning Rest the chief is that Rest is not needed for all effort therein. Thus one man at leisure will obtain work of another for many days without a sufficiency of Rest for that other and think to profit by this. So he may: but he profits singly, and when many rich do so by the poor it is like one eating his own flesh, since the withdrawal of Rest from those that labour will soon eat up the Commonwealth itself.

Much that men do with most anxiety is for the establishment of Rest. Wise men have often ordered gardens carefully for years, in order to enjoy Rest at last. Beds also are devised best when they give the deepest interval of repose and are surrounded by artifice with prolonged silence made of quiet strong wood and well curtained from the morning light. It is so with rooms removed from the other rooms of a house, and with days set apart from labour, and with certain kinds of companionship.

Undoubtedly the regimen of Rest for men is that of sleep, and sleep is a sort of medicine to Rest, and again a true expression of it. For though these two, Rest and Sleep, are not the same, yet without sleep no man can think of Rest, nor has Rest any one better body or way of being than this thing Sleep. For in Sleep a man utterly sinks down in proportion as it is deep and good into the centre of things and becomes one with that from which he came, drawing strength not only by negation from repose, but in some way positive from the being of his mother which is the earth. Some say that sleep is better near against the ground on this account, and all men know that sleep in wild places and without cover is the surest and the best. Sleep promises waking as Rest does a renewal of power; and the good dreams that come to us in sleep are a proof that in sleep we are still living.

A man may deny himself any other voluptuousness but not Rest. He may forego wine or flesh or anything of the body, and music or disputation, or anything of the mind, or love itself, or even companionship; but not Rest, for if he denies himself this he wastes himself and is himself no longer. Rest, therefore, is a necessary intermittent which we must have both for soul and body, and is the only necessity inherent to both those two so long as these two are bound together in the matter and net of this world. For food is a necessity to the body and virtue to the soul, but Rest to one and to the other.

There is no picture of delight in which we envy other men so much as when, lacking Rest, we see them possessing it; on which occasions we call out unwisely for a Perpetual Rest and for the cessation of all endeavour. In the same way men devise a lack of Rest for a special torment, and none can long survive it.

Rest and innocence are good fellows, and Rest is easier to the innocent man. The wicked suffer unrest always in some sort on account of God's presence warning them, though this unrest is stronger and much more to their good if men also warn them and if they live among such fellows in their commonwealth as will not permit their wickedness to be hidden or to go unpunished.

Rest has no time, and in its perfection must lose all mark of time. So a man sleeping deeply knows not how many hours have passed since he fell asleep until he awake again.

There are many good accompaniments for Rest, slow and distant music which at last is stiller and then silent; the scent of certain herbs and flowers and particularly of roses; clean linen; a pure clear air and the coming of night. To all these things prayer, an honourable profession and a preparation of the mind are in general a great aid, and, in the heat of the season, cool water refreshed with essences. A man also should make his toilet for Rest if he would have it full and thorough and prepare his body as his soul for a relaxation. He does well also in the last passage of his mind into sleep to commend himself to the care of God; remembering both how petty are all human vexations and also how weather-cock they are, turning now a face of terror and then in a moment another face of laughter or of insignificance. Many troubles that seem giants at evening are but dwarfs at sunrise, and some most terrific prove ghosts which speed off with the broadening of the day.

SENECA THE YOUNGER

# Of Peace of Mind

## I. [Serenus.]

When I examine myself, Seneca, some vices appear on the surface, and so that I can lay my hands upon them, while others are less distinct and harder to reach, and some are not always present, but recur at intervals: and these I should call the most troublesome, being like a roving enemy that assails one when he sees his opportunity, and who will neither let one stand on one's guard as in war, nor yet take one's rest without fear as in peace. The position in which I find myself more especially (for why should I not tell you the truth as I would to a physician), is that of neither being thoroughly set free from the vices which I fear and hate, nor yet quite in bondage to them: my state of mind, though not the worst possible, is a particularly discontented and sulky one: I am neither ill nor well. It is of no use for you to tell me that all virtues are weakly at the outset, and that they acquire strength and solidity by time, for I am well aware that even those which do but help our outward show, such as grandeur, a reputation for eloquence, and everything that appeals to others, gain power by time. Both those which afford us real strength and those which do but trick us out in a more attractive form, require long years before they gradually are adapted to us by time. But I fear that custom, which confirms most things, implants this vice more and more deeply in me. Long acquaintance with both good and bad people leads one to esteem them all alike. What this state of weakness really is, when the mind halts between two opinions without any strong inclination towards either good or evil, I shall be better able to show you piecemeal than all at once. I will tell you what befalls me, you must find out the name of the disease. I have to confess the greatest possible love of thrift: I do not care for a bed with gorgeous hangings, nor for clothes brought out of a chest, or pressed under weights and made glossy by frequent manglings, but for common and cheap ones, that require no care either to keep them or to put them on. For food I do not want what needs whole troops of

servants to prepare it and admire it, nor what is
ordered many days before and served up by many
hands, but something handy and easily come at,
with nothing far-fetched or costly about it, to be
had in every part of the world, burdensome neither to one's fortune nor one's body, not likely to
go out of the body by the same path by which it
came in. I like a rough and unpolished homebred
servant, I like my servant born in my house: I like
my country-bred father's heavy silver plate
stamped with no maker's name: I do not want a
table that is beauteous with dappled spots, or
known to all the town by the number of fashionable people to whom it has successively belonged,
but one which stands merely for use, and which
causes no guest's eye to dwell upon it with pleasure or to kindle at it with envy. While I am well
satisfied with this, I am reminded of the clothes
of a certain schoolboy, dressed with no ordinary
care and splendour, of slaves bedecked with gold
and a whole regiment of glittering attendants. I
think of houses too, where one treads on precious
stones, and where valuables lie about in every
corner, where the very roof is brilliantly painted,
and a whole nation attends and accompanies an
inheritance on the road to ruin. What shall I say
of waters, transparent to the very bottom, which

flow round the guests, and banquets worthy of the theatre in which they take place? Coming as I do from a long course of dull thrift, I find myself surrounded by the most brilliant luxury, which echoes around me on every side: my sight becomes a little dazzled by it: I can lift up my heart against it more easily than my eyes. When I return from seeing it I am a sadder, though not a worse man, I cannot walk amid my own paltry possessions with so lofty a step as before, and silently there steals over me a feeling of vexation, and a doubt whether that way of life may not be better than mine. None of these things alter my principles, yet all of them disturb me. At one time I would obey the maxims of our school and plunge into public life, I would obtain office and become consul, not because the purple robe and lictor's axes attract me, but in order that I may be able to be of use to my friends, my relatives, to all my countrymen, and indeed to all mankind. Ready and determined, I follow the advice of Zeno, Cleanthes, and Chrysippus, all of whom bid one take part in public affairs, though none of them ever did so himself: and then, as soon as something disturbs my mind, which is not used to receiving shocks, as soon as something occurs which is either disgraceful, such as often occurs in all men's lives, or which does not proceed quite easily, or when subjects of very little importance require me to devote a great deal of time to them, I go back to my life of leisure, and, just as even tired cattle go faster when they are going home, I wish to retire and pass my life within the walls of my house. "No one," I say, "that will give me no compensation worth such a loss shall ever rob me of a day. Let my mind be contained within itself and improve itself: let it take no part with other men's affairs, and do nothing which depends on the approval of others: let me enjoy a tranquility undisturbed by either public or private troubles." But whenever my spirit is roused by reading some brave words, or some noble example spurs me into action, I want to rush into the law courts, to place my voice at one man's disposal, my services at another's, and to try to help him even though I may not succeed, or to quell the pride of some lawyer who is puffed up by ill-deserved success: but I think, by Hercules, that in philosophical speculation it is better to view things as they are, and to speak of them on their own account, and as for words, to trust to things for them, and to let one's speech, simply follow whither they lead. "Why do you want to construct a fabric that will endure for ages? Do you not wish to do this in order that posterity may talk of you: yet you were born to die, and a silent death is the least wretched. Write something therefore in a simple style, merely to pass the time, for your own use, and not for publication. Less labour is needed when one does not look beyond the present." Then again, when the mind is elevated by the greatness of its thoughts, it becomes ostentatious in its use of words, the loftier its aspirations, the more loftily it desires to express them, and its speech rises to the dignity of its subject. At such times I forget my mild and moderate determination and soar higher than is my wont, using a language that is not my own. Not to multiply examples, I am in all things attended by this weakness of a well-meaning mind, to whose level I fear that I shall be gradually brought down, or what is even more worrying, that I may always hang as though about to fall, and that there may be more the matter with me than I myself perceive: for we take a friendly view of our own private affairs, and partiality always obscures our judgment. I fancy that many men would have arrived at wisdom had they not believed themselves to have arrived there already, had they not purposely deceived themselves as to some parts of their character, and passed by others with their eyes shut: for you have no grounds for supposing that other people's flattery is more ruinous to us than our own. Who dares to tell himself the truth? Who is there, by however large a troop of caressing courtiers he may be surrounded, who in spite of them is not his own greatest flatterer? I beg you, therefore, if you have any remedy by which you could stop this vacillation of mine, to deem me worthy to owe my peace of mind to you. I am well aware that these oscillations of mind are not perilous and that they threaten me with no serious disorder: to express what I complain of by an exact simile, I am not suffering from a storm, but from sea-sickness. Take from me, then, this evil, whatever it may be, and help one who is in distress within sight of land.

## II. [Seneca]

I have long been silently asking myself, my friend Serenus, to what I should liken such a condition of mind, and I find that nothing more closely resembles it than the conduct of those who, after having recovered from a long and serious illness, occasionally experience slight touches and twinges, and, although they have passed through the final stages of the disease, yet have suspicions that it has not left them, and though in perfect health yet hold out their pulse to be felt by the physician, and whenever they feel warm suspect that the fever is returning. Such men, Serenus, are not unhealthy, but they are not accustomed to being healthy; just as even a quiet sea or lake nevertheless displays a certain amount of ripple when its waters are subsiding after a storm. What you need, therefore, is, not any of those harsher remedies to which allusion has been made, not that you should in some cases check yourself, in others be angry with yourself, in others sternly reproach yourself, but that you should adopt that which comes last in the list, have confidence in yourself, and believe that you are proceeding on the right path, without being led aside by the numerous divergent tracks of wanderers which cross it in every direction, some of them circling about the right path itself. What you desire, to be undisturbed, is a great thing, nay, the greatest thing of all, and one which raises a man almost to the level of a god. The Greeks call this calm steadiness of mind *euthymia*, and Democritus's treatise upon it is excellently written: I call it peace of mind: for there is no necessity for translating so exactly as to copy the words of the Greek idiom: the essential point is to mark the matter under discussion by a name which ought to have the same meaning as its Greek name, though perhaps not the same form. What we are seeking, then, is how the mind may always pursue a steady, unruffled course, may be pleased with itself, and look with pleasure upon its surroundings, and experience no interruption of this joy, but abide in a peaceful condition without being ever either elated or depressed: this will be "peace of mind." Let us now consider in a general way how it may be attained: then you may apply as much as you choose of the universal remedy to your own case. Meanwhile we must drag to light the entire disease, and then each one will recognize his own part of it: at the same time you will understand how much less you suffer by your self-depreciation than those who are bound by some showy declaration which they have made, and are oppressed by some grand title of honour, so that shame rather than their own free will forces them to keep up the pretence. The same thing applies both to those who suffer from fickleness and continual changes of purpose, who always are fondest of what they have given up, and those who merely yawn and dawdle: add to these those who, like bad sleepers, turn from side to side, and settle themselves first in one manner and then in another, until at last they find rest through sheer weariness: in forming the habits of their lives they often end by adopting some to which they are not kept by any dislike of change, but in the practice of which old age, which is slow to alter, has caught them living: add also those who are by no means fickle, yet who must thank their dullness, not their consistency for being so, and who go on living not in the way they wish, but in the way they have begun to live. There are other special forms of this disease without number, but it has but one effect, that of making people dissatisfied with themselves. This arises from a distemperature of mind and from desires which one is afraid to express or unable to fulfill, when men either dare not attempt as much as they wish to do, or fail in their efforts and depend entirely upon hope: such people are always fickle and changeable, which is a necessary conse-quence of living in a state of suspense: they take any way to arrive at their ends, and teach and force themselves to use both dishonourable and difficult means to do so, so that when their toil has been in vain they are made wretched by the disgrace of failure, and do not regret having longed for what was wrong, but having longed for it in vain. They then begin to feel sorry for what they have done, and afraid to begin again, and their mind falls by degrees into a state of endless vacillation, because they can neither command nor obey their passions, of hesitation, because their life cannot properly develop itself, and of decay, as the mind becomes stupefied by disappointments. All these symptoms become aggravated when their dislike of a laborious misery has driven them to idleness and to secret studies, which are unendurable to a mind eager to take part in public affairs, desirous of action and naturally restless, because, of course, it finds too few resources within itself: when therefore it loses the amusement which business itself affords to busy men, it cannot endure home, loneliness, or the walls of a room, and regards itself with dislike when left to itself. Hence arises that weariness and dissatisfaction with oneself, that tossing to and fro of a mind which can nowhere find rest, that unhappy and unwilling endurance of enforced leisure. In all cases where one feels ashamed to confess the real cause of one's suffering, and where modesty leads one to drive one's sufferings inward, the desires pent up in a little space without any vent choke one another. Hence comes melancholy and drooping of spirit, and a thousand waverings of the unsteadfast mind, which is held in suspense by unfulfilled hopes, and saddened by disappointed ones: hence comes the state of mind of those who loathe their idleness, complain that they have nothing to do, and view the progress of others with the bitterest jealousy: for an unhappy sloth favours the growth of envy, and men who cannot succeed themselves wish every one else to be ruined. This dislike of other men's progress and despair of one's own produces a mind angered against fortune, addicted to complaining of the age in which it lives, to retiring into corners and brooding over its misery, until it becomes sick and weary of itself: for the human mind is naturally nimble and apt at movement: it delights in every opportunity of excitement and forgetfulness of itself, and the worse a man's disposition the more he delights in this, because he likes to wear himself out with busy action, just as some sores long for the hands that injure them and delight in being touched, and the foul itch enjoys anything that scratches it. Similarly I assure you that these minds, over which desires have spread like evil ulcers, take pleasure in toils and troubles, for there are some things which please our body while at the same time they give it a certain amount of pain, such as turning oneself over and changing one's side before it is wearied, or cooling oneself in one position after another. It is like Homer's Achilles, lying first upon its face, then upon its back, placing itself in various attitudes, and, as sick people are wont, enduring none of them for long, and using changes as though they were remedies. Hence men undertake aimless wanderings, travel along distant shores, and at one time at sea, at another by land, try to soothe that fickleness of disposition which always is dissatisfied with the present. "Now let us make for Campania: now I am sick of rich cultivation: let us see wild regions, let us thread the passes of Bruttii and Lucania: yet amid this wilderness one wants some thing of beauty to relieve our pampered eyes after so long dwelling on savage wastes: let us seek Tarentum with its famous harbour, its mild winter climate, and its district, rich enough to support even the great hordes of ancient times. Let us now return to town: our ears have too long missed its shouts and noise: it would be pleasant also to enjoy the sight of human bloodshed." Thus one journey succeeds another, and one sight is changed for another. As Lucretius says:—

*"Thus every mortal from himself doth flee;"*

but what does he gain by so doing if he does not escape from himself? he follows himself and weighs himself down by his own most burdensome companionship. We must understand, therefore, that what we suffer from is not the fault of the places but of ourselves: we are weak when there is anything to be endured, and cannot support either labour or pleasure, either one's own business or any one else's for long. This has driven some men to death, because by frequently altering their purpose they were always brought back to the same point, and had left themselves no room for anything new. They had become sick of life and of the world itself, and as all indulgences palled upon them they began to ask themselves the question, "How long are we to go on doing the same thing?"

III.

You ask me what I think we had better make use of to help us to support this ennui. "The best thing," as Athenodorus says, "is to occupy oneself with business, with the management of affairs of state and the duties of a citizen: for as some pass the day in exercising themselves in the sun and in taking care of their bodily health, and athletes find it most useful to spend the greater part of their time in feeding up the muscles and strength to whose cultivation they have devoted their lives; so too for you who are training your mind to take part in the struggles of political life, it is far more honourable to be thus at work than to be idle. He whose object is to be of service to his countrymen and to all mortals, exercises himself and does good at the same time when he is engrossed in business and is working to the best of his ability both in the interests of the public and of private men. But," continues he, "because innocence is hardly safe among such furious ambitions and so many men who turn one aside from the right path, and it is always sure to meet with more hindrance than help, we ought to withdraw ourselves from the forum and from public life, and a great mind even in a private station can find room wherein to expand freely. Confinement in dens restrains the springs of lions and wild creatures, but this does not apply to human beings, who often effect the most important works in retirement. Let a man, however, withdraw himself only in such a fashion that wherever he spends his leisure his wish may still be to benefit individual men and mankind alike, both with his intellect, his voice, and his advice.

The man that does good service to the state is not only he who brings forward candidates for public office, defends accused persons, and gives his vote on questions of peace and war, but he who encourages young men in well-doing, who supplies the present dearth of good teachers by instilling into their minds the principles of virtue, who seizes and holds back those who are rushing wildly in pursuit of riches and luxury, and, if he does nothing else, at least checks their course—such a man does service to the public though in a private station. Which does the most good, he who decides between foreigners and citizens (as praetor peregrinus), or, as praetor urbanus, pronounces sentence to the suitors in his court at his assistant's dictation, or he who shows them what is meant by justice, filial feeling, endurance, courage, contempt of death and knowledge of the gods, and how much a man is helped by a good conscience? If then you transfer to philosophy the time which you take away from the public service, you will not be a deserter or have refused to perform your proper task. A soldier is not merely one who stands in the ranks and defends the right or the left wing of the army, but he also who guards the gates—a service which, though less dangerous, is no sinecure—who keeps watch, and takes charge of the arsenal: though all these are blood-less duties, yet they count as military service. As soon as you have devoted yourself to philosophy, you will have overcome all disgust at life: you will not wish for darkness because you are weary of the light, nor will you be a trouble to your-self and useless to others: you will acquire many friends, and all the best men will be attracted towards you: for virtue, in however obscure a position, cannot be hidden, but gives signs of its presence: any one who is worthy will trace it out by its footsteps: but if we give up all society, turn our backs upon the whole human race, and live communing with ourselves alone, this solitude without any interesting occupation will lead to a want of something to do: we shall begin to build up and to pull down, to dam out the sea, to cause waters to flow through natural obstacles, and gen-erally to make a bad disposal of the time which Nature has given us to spend: some of us use it grudgingly, others wastefully; some of us spend it so that we can show a profit and loss account, others so that they have no assets remaining: than which nothing can be more shameful. Often a man who is very old in years has nothing beyond his age by which he can prove that he has lived a long time."

IV.

To me, my dearest Serenus, Athenodorus seems
to have yielded too completely to the times, to
have fled too soon: I will not deny that sometimes
one must retire, but one ought to retire slowly,
at a foot's pace, without losing one's ensigns or
one's honour as a soldier: those who make terms
with arms in their hands are more respected by
their enemies and more safe in their hands. This
is what I think ought to be done by virtue and by
one who practises virtue: if Fortune get the upper
hand and deprive him of the power of action, let
him not straightway turn his back to the enemy,
throw away his arms, and run away seeking for a
hiding-place, as if there were any place whither
Fortune could not pursue him, but let him be
more sparing in his acceptance of public office,
and after due deliberation discover some means
by which he can be of use to the state. He is not
able to serve in the army: then let him become
a candidate for civic honours: must he live in a
private station? then let him be an advocate: is he
condemned to keep silence? then let him help his
countrymen with silent counsel. Is it dangerous
for him even to enter the forum? then let him
prove himself a good comrade, a faithful friend,

a sober guest in people's houses, at public shows, and at wine-parties. Suppose that he has lost the status of a citizen; then let him exercise that of a man: our reason for magnanimously refusing to confine ourselves within the walls of one city, for having gone forth to enjoy intercourse with all lands and for professing ourselves to be citizens of the world is that we may thus obtain a wider theatre on which to display our virtue. Is the bench of judges closed to you, are you forbidden to address the people from the hustings, or to be a candidate at elections? then turn your eyes away from Rome, and see what a wide extent of territory, what a number of nations present themselves before you. Thus, it is never possible for so many outlets to be closed against your ambition that more will not remain open to it: but see whether the whole prohibition does not arise from your own fault. You do not choose to direct the affairs of the state except as consul or prytanis or meddix or sufes: what should we say if you refused to serve in the army save as general or military tribune? Even though others may form the first line, and your lot may have placed you among the veterans of the third, do your duty there with your voice, encouragement, example, and spirit: even though a man's hands be cut off, he may find means to help his side in a battle, if he stands his ground and cheers on his comrades. Do something of that sort yourself: if Fortune removes you from the front rank, stand your ground nevertheless and cheer on your comrades, and if somebody stops your mouth, stand nevertheless and help your side in silence. The services of a good citizen are never thrown away: he does good by being heard and seen, by his expression, his gestures, his silent determination, and his very walk. As some remedies benefit us by their smell as well as by their taste and touch, so virtue even when concealed and at a distance sheds usefulness around. Whether she moves at her ease and enjoys her just rights, or can only appear abroad on sufferance and is forced to shorten sail to the tempest, whether it be unemployed, silent, and pent up in a narrow lodging, or openly displayed, in whatever guise she may appear, she always does good. What? do you think that the example of one who can rest nobly has no value? It is by far the best plan, therefore, to mingle leisure with business, whenever chance impediments or the state of public affairs forbid one's leading an active life: for one is never so cut off from all pursuits as to find no room left for honourable action.

## V

Could you anywhere find a miserable city than that of Athens when it was being torn to pieces by the thirty tyrants? they slew thirteen hundred citizens, all the best men, and did not leave off because they had done so, but their cruelty became stimulated by exercise. In the city which possessed that most reverend tribunal, the Court of the Areopagus, which possessed a Senate, and a popular assembly which was like a Senate, there met daily a wretched crew of butchers, and the unhappy Senate House was crowded with tyrants. A state, in which there were so many tyrants that they would have been enough to form a bodyguard for one, might surely have rested from the struggle; it seemed impossible for men's minds even to conceive hopes of recovering their liberty, nor could they see any room for a remedy for such a mass of evil: for whence could the unhappy state obtain all the Harmodiuses it would need to slay so many tyrants? Yet Socrates was in the midst of the city, and consoled its mourning Fathers, encouraged those who despaired of the republic, by his reproaches brought rich men, who feared that their wealth would be their ruin, to a tardy repentance of their avarice, and moved about as a great example to those who wished to imitate him, because he walked a free man in the midst of thirty masters. However, Athens herself put him to death in prison, and Freedom herself could not endure the freedom of one who had treated a whole band of tyrants with scorn: you may know, therefore, that even in an oppressed state a wise man can find an opportunity for bringing himself to the front, and that in a prosperous and flourishing one wanton insolence, jealousy, and a thousand other cowardly vices bear sway. We ought, therefore, to expand or contract ourselves according as the state presents itself to us, or as Fortune offers us opportunities: but in any case we ought to move and not to become frozen still by fear: nay, he is the best man who, though peril menaces him on every side and arms and chains beset his path, nevertheless neither impairs nor conceals his virtue: for to keep oneself safe does not mean to bury oneself. I think that Curius Dentatus spoke truly when he said that he would rather be dead than alive: the worst evil of all is to leave the ranks of the living before one dies; yet it is your duty, if you happen to live in an age when it is not easy to serve the state, to devote more time to leisure and to literature. Thus, just as though you were making a perilous voyage, you may from time to time put into harbour, and set yourself free from public business without waiting for it to do so.

VI.

We ought, however, first to examine our own selves, next the business which we propose to transact, next those for whose sake or in whose company we transact it.

It is above all things necessary to form a true estimate of oneself, because as a rule we think that we can do more than we are able: one man is led too far through confidence in his eloquence, another demands more from his estate than it can produce, another burdens a weakly body with some toilsome duty. Some men are too shamefaced for the conduct of public affairs, which require an unblushing front: some men's obstinate pride renders them unfit for courts: some cannot control their anger, and break into unguarded language on the slightest provocation: some cannot rein in their wit or resist making risky jokes: for all these men leisure is better than employment: a bold, haughty and impatient nature ought to avoid anything that may lead it to use a freedom of speech which will bring it to ruin.

Next we must form an estimate of the matter which we mean to deal with, and compare our strength with the deed we are about to attempt: for the bearer ought always to be more powerful than his load: indeed, loads which are too heavy for their bearer must of necessity crush him: some affairs also are not so important in themselves as they are prolific and lead to much more business, which employments, as they involve us in new and various forms of work, ought to be refused. Neither should you engage in anything from which you are not free to retreat: apply yourself to something which you can finish, or at any rate can hope to finish: you had better not meddle with those operations which grow in importance, while they are being transacted, and which will not stop where you intended them to stop.

VII.

In all cases one should be careful in one's choice of men, and see whether they be worthy of our bestowing a part of our life upon them, or whether we shall waste our own time and theirs also: for some even consider us to be in their debt because of our services to them. Athenodorus said that "he would not so much as dine with a man who would not be grateful to him for doing so": meaning, I imagine, that much less would he go to dinner with those who recompense the services of their friends by their table, and regard courses of dishes as donatives, as if they overate themselves to do honour to others. Take away from these men their witnesses and spectators: they will take no pleasure in solitary gluttony. You must decide whether your disposition is better suited for vigorous action or for tranquil speculation and contemplation, and you must adopt whichever the bent of your genius inclines you for. Isocrates laid hands upon Ephorus and led him away from the forum, thinking that he would be more usefully employed in compiling chronicles; for no good is done by forcing one's mind to engage in uncongenial work: it is vain to struggle against Nature. Yet nothing delights the mind so much as faithful and pleasant friendship: what a blessing it is when there is one whose breast is ready to receive all your secrets with safety, whose knowledge of your actions you fear less than your own conscience, whose conversation removes your anxieties, whose advice assists your plans, whose cheerfulness dispels your gloom, whose very sight delights you! We should choose for our friends men who are, as far as possible, free from strong desires: for vices are contagious, and pass from a man to his neighbour, and injure those who touch them. As, therefore, in times of pestilence we have to be careful not to sit near people who are infected and in whom the disease is raging, because by so doing, we shall run into danger and catch the plague from their very breath; so, too, in choosing our friends' dispositions, we must take care to select those who are as far as may be unspotted by the world; for the way to breed disease is to mix what is sound with what is rotten. Yet I do not advise you to follow after or draw to yourself no one except a wise man: for where will you find him whom for so many centuries we have sought in vain? in the place of the best possible man take him who is least bad. You would hardly find any time that would have enabled you to make a happier choice than if you could have sought for a good man from among the Platos and Xenophons and the rest of the produce of the brood of Socrates, or if you had been permitted to choose one from the age of Cato: an age which bore many men worthy to be born in Cato's time (just as it also bore many men worse than were ever known before, planners of the blackest crimes: for it needed both classes in order to make Cato understood:

it wanted both good men, that he might win their approbation, and bad men, against whom he could prove his strength): but at the present day, when there is such a dearth of good men, you must be less squeamish in your choice. Above all, however, avoid dismal men who grumble at whatever happens, and find something to complain of in everything. Though he may continue loyal and friendly towards you, still one's peace of mind is destroyed by a comrade whose mind is soured and who meets every incident with a groan.

## VIII.

Let us now pass on to the consideration of property, that most fertile source of human sorrows: for if you compare all the other ills from which we suffer—deaths, sicknesses, fears, regrets, endurance of pains and labours – with those miseries which our money inflicts upon us, the latter will far outweigh all the others. Reflect, then, how much less a grief it is never to have had any money than to have lost it: we shall thus understand that the less poverty has to lose, the less torment it has with which to afflict us: for you are mistaken if you suppose that the rich bear their losses with greater spirit than the poor: a wound causes the same amount of pain to the greatest and the smallest body. It was a neat saying of Bion's, "that it hurts bald men as much as hairy men to have their hairs pulled out": you may be assured that the same thing is true of rich and poor people, that their suffering is equal: for their money clings to both classes, and cannot be torn away without their feeling it: yet it is more endurable, as I have said, and easier not to gain property than to lose it, and therefore you will find that those upon whom Fortune has never smiled are more cheerful than those whom she has deserted. Diogenes, a man of infinite spirit, perceived this, and made it impossible that anything should be taken from him. Call this security from loss poverty, want, necessity, or any contemptuous name you please: I shall consider such a man to be happy, unless you find me another who can lose nothing. If I am not mistaken, it is a royal attribute among so many misers, sharpers, and robbers, to be the one man who cannot be injured. If any one doubts the happiness of Diogenes, he would doubt whether the position of the immortal gods was one of sufficient happiness, because they have no farms or gardens, no valuable estates let to strange tenants, and no large loans in the money market. Are you not ashamed of yourself, you who gaze upon riches with astonished admiration? Look upon the universe: you will see the gods quite bare of property, and possessing nothing though they give everything. Do you think that this man who has stripped himself of all fortuitous accessories is a pauper, or one like to the immortal gods? Do you call Demetrius, Pompeius's freedman, a happier man, he who was not ashamed to be richer than Pompeius, who was daily furnished with a list of the number of his slaves, as a general is with that of his army, though he had long deserved that all his riches should consist of a pair of underlings, and a roomier cell than the other slaves? But Diogenes's only slave ran away from him, and when he was pointed out to Diogenes, he did not think him worth fetching back. "It is a shame," he said, "that Manes should be able to live without Diogenes, and that Diogenes should not be able to live without Manes." He seems to me to have said, "Fortune, mind your own business: Diogenes has nothing left that belongs to you. Did my slave run away? nay, he went away from me as a free man." A household of slaves requires food and clothing: the bellies of so many hungry creatures have to be filled: we must buy raiment for them, we must watch their most thievish hands, and we must make use of the services of people who weep and execrate us. How far happier is he who is indebted to no man for anything except for what he can deprive himself of with the greatest ease! Since we, however, have not such strength of mind as this, we ought at any rate to diminish the extent of our property, in order to be less exposed to the assaults of fortune: those men whose bodies can be within the shelter of their armour, are more fitted for war than those whose huge size everywhere extends beyond it, and exposes them to wounds: the best amount of property to have is that which is enough to keep us from poverty, and which yet is not far removed from it.

IX.

We shall be pleased with this measure of wealth if we have previously taken pleasure in thrift, without which no riches are sufficient, and with which none are insufficient, especially as the remedy is always at hand, and poverty itself by calling in the aid of thrift can convert itself into riches. Let us accustom ourselves to set aside mere outward show, and to measure things by their uses, not by their ornamental trappings: let our hunger be tamed by food, our thirst quenched by drinking, our lust confined within needful bounds; let us learn to use our limbs, and to arrange our dress and way of life according to what was approved of by our ancestors, not in imitation of new-fangled models: let us learn to increase our continence, to repress luxury, to set bounds to our pride, to assuage our anger, to look upon poverty without prejudice, to practise thrift, albeit many are ashamed to do so, to apply cheap remedies to the wants of nature, to keep all undisciplined hopes and aspirations as it were under lock and key, and to make it our business to get our riches from ourselves and not from Fortune. We never can so thoroughly defeat the vast diversity and malignity of misfortune with which we are threatened as not to feel the weight of many gusts if we offer a large spread of canvas to the wind: we must draw our affairs into a small compass, to make the darts of Fortune of no avail. For this reason, sometimes slight mishaps have turned into remedies, and more serious disorders have been healed by slighter ones. When the mind pays no attention to good advice, and cannot be brought to its senses by milder measures, why should we not think that its interests are being served by poverty, disgrace, or financial ruin being applied to it? one evil is balanced by another. Let us then teach ourselves to be able to dine without all Rome to look on, to be the slaves of fewer slaves, to get clothes which fulfill their original purpose, and to live in a smaller house. The inner curve is the one to take, not only in running races and in the contests of the circus, but also in the race of life; even literary pursuits, the most becoming thing for a gentleman to spend money upon, are only justifiable as long as they are kept within bounds. What is the use of possessing numberless books and libraries, whose titles their owner can hardly read through in a lifetime? A student is over-whelmed by such a mass, not instructed, and it is much better to devote yourself to a few writers than to skim through many. Forty thousand books were burned at Alexandria: some would have praised this library as a most noble memorial of royal wealth, like Titus Livius, who says that it was "a splendid result of the taste and attentive care of the kings." It had nothing to do with taste or care, but was a piece of learned luxury, nay, not even learned, since they amassed it, not for the sake of learning, but to make a show, like many men who know less about letters than a slave is expected to know, and who uses his books not to help him in his studies but to ornament his dining-room. Let a man, then, obtain as many books as he wants, but none for show. "It is more respectable," say you, "to spend one's money on such books than on vases of Corinthian brass and paintings." Not so: everything that is carried to excess is wrong. What excuses can you find for a man who is eager to buy bookcases of ivory and citrus wood, to collect the works of unknown or discredited authors, and who sits yawning amid so many thousands of books, whose backs and titles please him more than any other part of them? Thus in the houses of the laziest of men you will see the works of all the orators and historians stacked upon bookshelves reaching right up to the ceiling. At the present day a library has become as necessary an appendage to a house as a hot and cold bath. I would excuse them straightway if they really were carried away by an excessive zeal for literature; but as it is, these costly works of sacred genius, with all the illustrations that adorn them, are merely bought for display and to serve as wall-furniture.

X.

Suppose, however, that your life has become full of trouble, and that without knowing what you were doing you have fallen into some snare which either public or private Fortune has set for you, and that you can neither untie it nor break it: then remember that fettered men suffer much at first from the burdens and clogs upon their legs: afterwards, when they have made up their minds not to fret themselves about them, but to endure them, necessity teaches them to bear them bravely, and habit to bear them easily. In every station of life you will find amusements, relaxations, and enjoyments; that is, provided you be willing to make light of evils rather than to hate them. Knowing to what sorrows we were born, there is nothing for which Nature more deserves our thanks than for having invented habit as an alleviation of misfortune, which soon accustoms us to the severest evils. No one could hold out against misfortune if it permanently exercised the same force as at its first onset. We are all chained to Fortune: some men's chain is loose and made of gold, that of others is tight and of meaner metal: but what difference does this make? we are all included in the same captivity, and even those who have bound us are bound themselves, unless you think that a chain on the left side is lighter to bear: one man may be bound by public office, another by wealth: some have to bear the weight of illustrious, some of humble birth: some are subject to the commands of others, some only to their own: some are kept in one place by being banished thither, others by being elected to the priesthood. All life is slavery: let each man therefore reconcile himself to his lot, complain of it as little as possible, and lay hold of whatever good lies within his reach. No condition can be so wretched that an impartial mind can find no compensations in it. Small sites, if ingeniously divided, may be made use of for many different purposes, and arrangement will render ever so narrow a room habitable. Call good sense to your aid against difficulties: it is possible to soften what is harsh, to widen what is too narrow, and to make heavy burdens press less severely upon one who bears them skillfully. Moreover, we ought not to allow our desires to wander far afield, but we must make them confine themselves to our immediate neighbourhood, since they will not endure to be altogether locked up. We must leave alone things which either cannot come to pass or can only be effected with difficulty, and follow after such things as are near at hand and within reach of our hopes, always remembering that all things are equally unimportant, and that though they have a different outward appearance, they are all alike empty within. Neither let us envy those who are in high places: the heights which look lofty to us are steep and rugged. Again, those whom unkind fate has placed in critical situations will be safer if they show as little pride in their proud position as may be, and do all they are able to bring down their fortunes to the level of other men's. There are many who must needs cling to their high pinnacle of power, because they cannot descend from it save by falling headlong: yet they assure us that their greatest burden is being obliged to be burdensome to others, and that they are nailed to their lofty post rather than raised to it: let them then, by dispensing justice, clemency, and kindness with an open and liberal hand, provide themselves with assistance to break their fall, and looking forward to this maintain their position more hopefully. Yet nothing sets us free from these alternations of hope and fear so well as always fixing some limit to our successes, and not allowing Fortune to choose when to stop our career, but to halt of our own accord long before we apparently need do so. By acting thus certain desires will rouse up our spirits, and yet being confined within bounds, will not lead us to embark on vast and vague enterprises.

# XI.

These remarks of mine apply only to imperfect, commonplace, and unsound natures, not to the wise man, who needs not to walk with timid and cautious gait: for he has such confidence in himself that he does not hesitate to go directly in the teeth of Fortune, and never will give way to her. Nor indeed has he any reason for fearing her, for he counts not only chattels, property, and high office, but even his body, his eyes, his hands, and everything whose use makes life dearer to us, nay, even his very self, to be things whose possession is uncertain; he lives as though he had borrowed them, and is ready to return them cheerfully whenever they are claimed. Yet he does not hold himself cheap, because he knows that he is not his own, but performs all his duties as carefully and prudently as a pious and scrupulous man would take care of property left in his charge as trustee. When he is bidden to give them up, he will not complain of Fortune, but will say, "I thank you for what I have had possession of: I have managed your property so as largely to increase it, but since you order me, I give it back to you and return it willingly and thankfully. If you still wish me to own anything of yours, I will keep it for you: if you have other views, I restore into your hands and make restitution of all my wrought and coined silver, my house and my household. Should Nature recall what she previously entrusted us with, let us say to her also: 'Take back my spirit, which is better than when you gave it me: I do not shuffle or hang back. Of my own free will I am ready to return what you gave me before I could think: take me away.'" What hardship can there be in returning to the place from whence one came? a man cannot live well if he knows not how to die well. We must, therefore, take away from this commodity its original value, and count the breath of life as a cheap matter. "We dislike gladiators," says Cicero, "if they are eager to save their lives by any means whatever: but we look favourably upon them if they are openly reckless of them." You may be sure that the same thing occurs with us: we often die because we are afraid of death. Fortune, which regards our lives as a show in the arena for her own enjoyment, says, "Why should I spare you, base and cowardly creature that you are? you will be pierced and hacked with all the more wounds because you know not how to offer your throat to the knife: whereas you, who receive the stroke without drawing away your neck or putting up your hands to stop it, shall both live longer and die more quickly." He who fears death will never act as becomes a living man: but he who knows that this fate was laid upon him as soon as he was conceived will live according to it, and by this strength of mind will gain this further advantage, that nothing can befall him unexpectedly: for by looking forward to everything which can happen as though it would happen to him, he takes the sting out of all evils, which can make no difference to those who expect it and are prepared to meet it: evil only comes hard upon those who have lived without giving it a thought and whose attention has been exclusively directed to happiness. Disease, captivity, disaster, conflagration, are none of them unexpected: I always knew with what disorderly company Nature had associated me. The dead have often been wailed for in my neighbourhood: the torch and taper have often been borne past my door before the bier of one who has died before his time: the crash of falling buildings has often resounded by my side: night has snatched away many of those with whom I have become intimate in the forum, the Senate-house, and in society, and has sundered the hands which were joined in friendship: ought I to be surprised if the dangers which have always been circling around me at last assail me? How large a part of mankind never think of storms when about to set sail? I shall never be ashamed to quote a good saying because it comes from a bad author. Publilius, who was a more powerful writer than any of our other playwrights, whether comic or tragic, whenever he chose to rise above farcical absurdities and speeches addressed to the gallery, among many other verses too noble even for tragedy, let alone for comedy, has this one:—

*"What one hath suffered may befall us all."*

If a man takes this into his inmost heart and looks upon all the misfortunes of other men, of which there is always a great plenty, in this spirit, remembering that there is nothing to prevent their coming upon him also, he will arm himself against them long before they attack him. It is too late to school the mind to endurance of peril after peril has come. "I did not think this would happen," and "Would you ever have believed that this would have happened?" say you. But why should it not? Where are the riches after which want, hunger, and beggary do not follow? what office is there whose purple robe, augur's staff,

and patrician reins have not as their accompani-
ment rags and banishment, the brand of infamy,
a thousand disgraces, and utter reprobation?
what kingdom is there for which ruin, trampling
under foot, a tyrant and a butcher are not ready
at hand? nor are these matters divided by long
periods of time, but there is but the space of an
hour between sitting on the throne ourselves and
clasping the knees of someone else as suppliants.
Know then that every station of life is transitory,
and that what has ever happened to anybody
may happen to you also. You are wealthy: are you
wealthier than Pompeius? Yet when Gaius, his
old relative and new host, opened Caesar's house
to him in order that he might close his own, he
lacked both bread and water: though he owned
so many rivers which both rose and discharged
themselves within his dominions, yet he had to
beg for drops of water: he perished of hunger and
thirst in the palace of his relative, while his heir
was contracting for a public funeral for one who
was in want of food. You have filled public offices:
were they either as important, as unlooked for,
or as all-embracing as those of Sejanus? Yet on
the day on which the Senate disgraced him, the
people tore him to pieces: the executioner could
find no part left large enough to drag to the Tiber,

of one upon whom gods and men had showered all that could be given to man. You are a king: I will not bid you go to Croesus for an example, he who while yet alive saw his funeral pile both lighted and extinguished, being made to outlive not only his kingdom but even his own death, nor to Jugurtha, whom the people of Rome beheld as a captive within the year in which they had feared him. We have seen Ptolemaeus King of Africa, and Mithridates King of Armenia, under the charge of Gaius's guards: the former was sent into exile, the latter chose it in order to make his exile more honourable. Among such continual topsy-turvy changes, unless you expect that whatever can happen will happen to you, you give adversity power against you, a power which can be destroyed by any one who looks at it beforehand.

XII.

The next point to these will be to take care that we do not labour for what is vain, or labour in vain: that is to say, neither to desire what we are not able to obtain, nor yet, having obtained our desire too late, and after much toil to discover the folly of our wishes: in other words, that our labour may not be without result, and that the result may not be unworthy of our labour: for as a rule sadness arises from one of these two things, either from want of success or from being ashamed of having succeeded. We must limit the running to and fro which most men practise, rambling about houses, theatres, and market-places. They mind other men's business, and always seem as though they themselves had something to do. If you ask one of them as he comes out of his own door, "Whither are you going?" he will answer, "By Hercules, I do not know: but I shall see some people and do something." They wander purposelessly seeking for something to do, and do, not what they have made up their minds to do, but what has casually fallen in their way. They move uselessly and without any plan, just like ants crawling over bushes, which creep up to the top and then down to the bottom again without gaining anything. Many men spend their lives in exactly the same fashion, which one may call a state of restless indolence. You would pity some of them when you see them running as if their house was on fire: they actually jostle all whom they meet, and hurry along themselves and others with them, though all the while they are are going to salute some one who will not return their greeting, or to attend the funeral of some one whom they did not know: they are going to hear the verdict on one who often goes to law, or to see the wedding of one who often gets married: they will follow a man's litter, and in some places will even carry it: afterwards returning home weary with idleness, they swear that they themselves do not know why they went out, or where they have been, and on the following day they will wander through the same round again. Let all your work, therefore, have some purpose, and keep some object in view: these restless people are not made restless by labour, but are driven out of their minds by mistaken ideas: for even they do not put themselves in motion without any hope: they are excited by the outward appearance of something, and their crazy mind cannot see its futility. In the same way every one of those who walk out to swell the crowd in the streets, is led round the city by worthless and empty reasons; the dawn drives him forth, although he has nothing to do, and after he has pushed his way into many men's doors, and saluted their nomenclators one after the other, and been turned away from many others, he finds that the most difficult person of all to find at home is himself. From this evil habit comes that worst of all vices, talebearing and prying into public and private secrets, and the knowledge of many things which it is neither safe to tell nor safe to listen to.

## XIII.

It was, I imagine, following out this principle that Democritus taught that "he who would live at peace must not do much business either public or private," referring of course to unnecessary business: for if there be any necessity for it we ought to transact not only much but endless business, both public and private; in cases, however, where no solemn duty invites us to act, we had better keep ourselves quiet: for he who does many things often puts himself in Fortune's power, and it is safest not to tempt her often, but always to remember her existence, and never to promise oneself anything on her security. I will set sail unless anything happens to prevent me, I shall be praetor, if nothing hinders me, my financial operations will succeed, unless anything goes wrong with them. This is why we say that nothing befals the wise man which he did not expect—we do not make him exempt from the chances of human life, but from its mistakes, nor does everything happen to him as he wished it would, but as he thought it would: now his first thought was that his purpose might meet with some resistance, and the pain of disappointed wishes must affect a man's mind less severely if he has not been at all events confident of success.

XIV.

Moreover, we ought to cultivate an easy temper, and not become over fond of the lot which fate has assigned to us, but transfer ourselves to whatever other condition chance may lead us to, and fear no alteration, either in our purposes or our position in life, provided that we do not become subject to caprice, which of all vices is the most hostile to repose: for obstinacy, from which Fortune often wrings some concession, must needs be anxious and unhappy, but caprice, which can never restrain itself, must be more so. Both of these qualities, both that of altering nothing, and that of being dissatisfied with everything, are enemies to repose. The mind ought in all cases to be called away from the contemplation of external things to that of itself: let it confide in itself, rejoice in itself, admire its own works; avoid as far as may be those of others, and devote itself to itself; let it not feel losses, and put a good construction even upon misfortunes. Zeno, the chief of our school, when he heard the news of a shipwreck, in which all his property had been lost, remarked, "Fortune bids me follow philosophy in lighter marching order." A tyrant threatened Theodorus with death, and even with want of burial. "You are able to please yourself," he answered, "my half pint of blood is in your power: for, as for burial, what a fool you must be if you suppose that I care whether I rot above ground or under it." Julius Kanus, a man of peculiar greatness, whom even the fact of his having been born in this century does not prevent our admiring, had a long dispute with Gaius, and when as he was going away that Phalaris of a man said to him, "That you may not delude yourself with any foolish hopes, I have ordered you to be executed," he answered, "I thank you, most excellent prince." I am not sure what he meant: for many ways of explaining his conduct occur to me. Did he wish to be reproachful, and to show him how great his cruelty must be if death became a kindness? or did he upbraid him with his accustomed insanity? for even those whose children were put to death, and whose goods were confiscated, used to thank him: or was it that he willingly received death, regarding it as freedom? Whatever he meant, it was a magnanimous answer. Some one may say, "After this Gaius might have let him live." Kanus had no fear of this: the good faith with which Gaius carried out such orders as these was well known. Will you believe that he passed the ten intervening days before his execution without the slightest despondency? it is marvellous how that man spoke and acted, and how peaceful he was. He was playing at draughts when the centurion in charge of a number of those who were going to be executed bade him, join them: on the summons he counted his men and said to his companion, "Mind you do not tell a lie after my death, and say that you won;" then, turning to the centurion, he said "You will bear me witness that I am one man ahead of him." Do you think that Kanus played upon that draught-board? nay, he played with it. His friends were sad at being about to lose so great a man: "Why," asked he, "are you sorrowful? you are enquiring whether our souls are immortal, but I shall presently know." Nor did he up to the very end cease his search after truth, and raised arguments upon the subject of his own death. His own teacher of philosophy accompanied him, and they were not far from the hill on which the daily sacrifice to Caesar our god was offered, when he said, "What are you thinking of now, Kanus? or what are your ideas?" "I have decided," answered Kanus, "at that most swiftly-passing moment of all to watch whether the spirit will be conscious of the act of leaving the body." He promised, too, that if he made any discoveries, he would come round to his friends and tell them what the condition of the souls of the departed might be. Here was peace in the very midst of the storm: here was a soul worthy of eternal life, which used its own fate as a proof of truth, which when at the last step of life experimented upon his fleeting breath, and did not merely continue to learn until he died, but learned something even from death itself. No man has carried the life of a philosopher further. I will not hastily leave the subject of a great man, and one who deserves to be spoken of with respect: I will hand thee down to all posterity, thou most noble heart, chief among the many victims of Gaius.

XV.

Yet we gain nothing by getting rid of all personal causes of sadness, for sometimes we are possessed by hatred of the human race. When you reflect how rare simplicity is, how unknown innocence, how seldom faith is kept, unless it be to our advantage, when you remember such numbers of successful crimes, so many equally hateful losses and gains of lust, and ambition so impatient even of its own natural limits that it is willing to purchase distinction by baseness, the mind seems as it were cast into darkness, and shadows rise before it as though the virtues were all overthrown and we were no longer allowed to hope to possess them or benefited by their possession. We ought therefore to bring ourselves into such a state of mind that all the vices of the vulgar may not appear hateful to us, but merely ridiculous, and we should imitate Democritus rather than Heraclitus. The latter of these, whenever he appeared in public, used to weep, the former to laugh: the one thought all human doings to be follies, the other thought them to be miseries. We must take a higher view of all things, and bear with them more easily: it better becomes a man to scoff at life than to lament over it. Add to this that he who laughs at the human race deserves better of it than he who mourns for it, for the former leaves it some good hopes of improvement, while the latter stupidly weeps over what he has given up all hopes of mending. He who after surveying the universe cannot control his laughter shows, too, a greater mind than he who cannot restrain his tears, because his mind is only affected in the slightest possible degree, and he does not think that any part of all this apparatus is either important, or serious, or unhappy. As for the several causes which render us happy or sorrowful, let everyone describe them for himself, and learn the truth of Bion's saying, "That all the doings of men were very like what he began with, and that there is nothing in their lives which is more holy or decent than their conception." Yet it is better to accept public morals and human vices calmly without bursting into either laughter or tears; for to be hurt by the sufferings of others is to be for ever miserable, while to enjoy the sufferings of others is an inhuman pleasure, just as it is a useless piece of humanity to weep and pull a long face because some one is burying his son. In one's own misfortunes, also, one ought so to conduct oneself as to bestow upon them just as much sorrow as reason, not as much as custom requires: for many shed tears in order to show them, and whenever no one is looking at them their eyes are dry, but they think it disgraceful not to weep when every one does so. So deeply has this evil of being guided by the opinion of others taken root in us, that even grief, the simplest of all emotions, begins to be counterfeited.

XVI.

There comes now a part of our subject which is wont with good cause to make one sad and anxious: I mean when good men come to bad ends; when Socrates is forced to die in prison, Rutilius to live in exile, Pompeius and Cicero to offer their necks to the swords of their own followers, when the great Cato, that living image of virtue, falls upon his sword and rips up both himself and the republic, one cannot help being grieved that Fortune should bestow her gifts so unjustly: what, too, can a good man hope to obtain when he sees the best of men meeting with the worst fates. Well, but see how each of them endured his fate, and if they endured it bravely, long in your heart for courage as great as theirs; if they died in a womanish and cowardly manner, nothing was lost: either they deserved that you should admire their courage, or else they did not deserve that you should wish to imitate their cowardice: for what can be more shameful than that the greatest men should die so bravely as to make people cowards. Let us praise one who deserves such constant praises, and say, "The braver you are the happier you are! You have escaped from all accidents, jealousies, diseases: you have escaped from prison: the gods have not thought you worthy of ill-fortune, but have thought that fortune no longer deserved to have any power over you": but when any one shrinks back in the hour of death and looks longingly at life, we must lay hands upon him. I will never weep for a man who dies cheerfully, nor for one who dies weeping: the former wipes away my tears, the latter by his tears makes himself unworthy that any should be shed for him. Shall I weep for Hercules because he was burned alive, or for Regulus because he was pierced by so many nails, or for Cato because he tore open his wounds a second time? All these men discovered how at the cost of a small portion of time they might obtain immortality, and by their deaths gained eternal life.

XVII.

It also proves a fertile source of troubles if you take pains to conceal your feelings and never show yourself to any one undisguised, but, as many men do, live an artificial life, in order to impose upon others: for the constant watching of himself becomes a torment to a man, and he dreads being caught doing something at variance with his usual habits, and, indeed, we never can

68

be at our ease if we imagine that everyone who looks at us is weighing our real value: for many things occur which strip people of their disguise, however reluctantly they may part with it, and even if all this trouble about oneself is successful, still life is neither happy nor safe when one always has to wear a mask. But what pleasure there is in that honest straight-forwardness which is its own ornament, and which conceals no part of its character? Yet even this life, which hides nothing from any one runs some risk of being despised; for there are people who disdain whatever they come close to: but there is no danger of virtue's becoming contemptible when she is brought near our eyes, and it is better to be scorned for one's simplicity than to bear the burden of unceasing hypocrisy. Still, we must observe moderation in this matter, for there is a great difference between living simply and living slovenly. Moreover, we ought to retire a great deal into ourselves: for association with persons unlike ourselves upsets all that we had arranged, rouses the passions which were at rest, and rubs into a sore any weak or imperfectly healed place in our minds. Nevertheless we ought to mix up these two things, and to pass our lives alternately in solitude and among throngs of people; for the former will make us long for the society of mankind, the latter for that of ourselves, and the one will counteract the other: solitude will cure us when we are sick of crowds, and crowds will cure us when we are sick of solitude. Neither ought we always to keep the mind strained to the same pitch, but it ought sometimes to be relaxed by amusement. Socrates did not blush to play with little boys, Cato used to refresh his mind with wine after he had wearied it with application to affairs of state, and Scipio would move his triumphal and soldierly limbs to the sound of music, not with a feeble and halting gait, as is the fashion now-a-days, when we sway in our very walk with more than womanly weakness, but dancing as men were wont in the days of old on sportive and festal occasions, with manly bounds, thinking it no harm to be seen so doing even by their enemies. Men's minds ought to have relaxation: they rise up better and more vigorous after rest. We must not force crops from rich fields, for an unbroken course of heavy crops will soon exhaust their fertility, and so also the liveliness of our minds will be destroyed by unceasing labour, but they will recover their strength after a short period of rest and relief: for continuous toil produces a sort of numbness and sluggishness. Men would not be so eager for this, if play and amusement did not possess natural attractions for them, although constant indulgence in them takes away all gravity and all strength from the mind: for sleep, also, is necessary for our refreshment, yet if you prolong it for days and nights together it will become death. There is a great difference between slackening your hold of a thing and letting it go. The founders of our laws appointed festivals, in order that men might be publicly encouraged to be cheerful, and they thought it necessary to vary our labours with amusements, and, as I said before, some great men have been wont to give themselves a certain number of holidays in every month, and some divided every day into play-time and work-time. Thus, I remember that great orator Asinius Pollio would not attend to any business after the tenth hour: he would not even read letters after that time for fear some new trouble should arise, but in those two hours used to get rid of the weariness which he had contracted during the whole day. Some rest in the middle of the day, and reserve some light occupation for the afternoon. Our ancestors, too, forbade any new motion to be made in the Senate after the tenth hour. Soldiers divide their watches, and those who have just returned from active service are allowed to sleep the whole night undisturbed. We must humour our minds and grant them rest from time to time, which acts upon them like food, and restores their strength. It does good also to take walks out of doors, that our spirits may be raised and refreshed by the open air and fresh breeze: sometimes we gain strength by driving in a carriage, by travel, by change of air, or by social meals and a more generous allowance of wine: at times we ought to drink even to intoxication, not so as to drown, but merely to dip ourselves in wine: for wine washes away troubles and dislodges them from the depths of the mind, and acts as a remedy to sorrow as it does to some diseases. The inventor of wine is called Liber, not from the licence which he gives to our tongues, but because he liberates the mind from the bondage of cares, and emancipates it, animates it, and renders it more daring in all that it attempts. Yet moderation is wholesome both in freedom and in wine. It is believed that Solon and Arcesilaus used to drink deep. Cato is reproached with drunkenness: but whoever casts this in his teeth will find it easier to turn his reproach into a commendation than to prove that Cato did anything wrong: however, we ought not to do it often, for fear the mind should contract evil habits, though it ought sometimes to be forced into frolic and frankness, and to cast off dull sobriety for a while. If we believe the Greek poet, "it is sometimes pleasant to be mad"; again, Plato always knocked in vain at the door of poetry when he was sober; or, if we trust Aristotle, no great genius has ever been without a touch of insanity. The mind cannot use lofty language, above that of the common herd, unless it be excited. When it has spurned aside the commonplace environments of custom, and rises sublime, instinct with sacred fire, then alone can it chant a song too grand for mortal lips: as long as it continues to dwell within itself it cannot rise to any pitch of splendour: it must break away from the beaten track, and lash itself to frenzy, till it gnaws the curb and rushes away bearing up its rider to heights whither it would fear to climb when alone.

I have now, my beloved Serenus, given you an account of what things can preserve peace of mind, what things can restore it to us, what can arrest the vices which secretly undermine it: yet be assured, that none of these is strong enough to enable us to retain so fleeting a blessing, unless we watch over our vacillating mind with intense and unremitting care.

# Peaceful
# Hours

OKAKURA KAKUZŌ

# The Cup of Humanity

Tea began as a medicine and grew into a beverage. In China, in the eighth century, it entered the realm of poetry as one of the polite amusements. The fifteenth century saw Japan ennoble it into a religion of aestheticism—Teaism. Teaism is a cult founded on the adoration of the beautiful among the sordid facts of everyday existence. It inculcates purity and harmony, the mystery of mutual charity, the romanticism of the social order. It is essentially a worship of the Imperfect, as it is a tender attempt to accomplish something possible in this impossible thing we know as life.

The Philosophy of Tea is not mere aestheticism in the ordinary acceptance of the term, for it expresses conjointly with ethics and religion our whole point of view about man and nature. It is hygiene, for it enforces cleanliness; it is economics, for it shows comfort in simplicity rather than in the complex and costly; it is moral geometry, inasmuch as it defines our sense of proportion to the universe. It represents the true spirit of Eastern democracy by making all its votaries aristocrats in taste.

The long isolation of Japan from the rest of the world, so conducive to introspection, has been highly favourable to the development of Teaism. Our home and habits, costume and cuisine, porcelain, lacquer, painting—our very literature—all have been subject to its influence. No student of Japanese culture could ever ignore its presence. It has permeated the elegance of noble boudoirs, and entered the abode of the humble. Our peasants have learned to arrange flowers, our meanest labourer to offer his salutation to the rocks and waters. In our common parlance we speak of the man "with no tea" in him, when he is insusceptible to the seriocomic interests of the personal drama. Again we stigmatise the untamed aesthete who, regardless of the mundane tragedy, runs riot in the springtide of emancipated emotions, as one "with too much tea" in him.

The outsider may indeed wonder at this seeming much ado about nothing. What a tempest in a tea-cup! he will say. But when we consider how small after all the cup of human enjoyment is, how soon overflowed with tears, how easily drained to the dregs in our quenchless thirst for infinity, we shall not blame ourselves for making so much of the tea-cup. Mankind has done worse. In the worship of Bacchus, we have sacrificed too freely; and we have even transfigured the gory image of Mars. Why not consecrate ourselves to the queen of the Camelias, and revel in the warm stream of sympathy that flows from her altar? In the liquid amber within the ivory-porcelain, the initiated may touch the sweet reticence of Confucius, the piquancy of Laotse, and the ethereal aroma of Sakyamuni himself.

Those who cannot feel the littleness of great things in themselves are apt to overlook the greatness of little things in others. The average Westerner, in his sleek complacency, will see in the tea ceremony but another instance of the thousand and one oddities which constitute the quaintness and childishness of the East to him. He was wont to regard Japan as barbarous while she indulged in the gentle arts of peace: he calls her civilised since she began to commit whole-sale slaughter on Manchurian battlefields. Much comment has been given lately to the Code of the Samurai,—the Art of Death which makes our soldiers exult in self-sacrifice; but scarcely any attention has been drawn to Teaism, which represents so much of our Art of Life. Fain would we remain barbarians, if our claim to civilisation were to be based on the gruesome glory of war. Fain would we await the time when due respect shall be paid to our art and ideals.

When will the West understand, or try to understand, the East? We Asiatics are often appalled by the curious web of facts and fancies which has been woven concerning us. We are pictured as living on the perfume of the lotus, if not on mice and cockroaches. It is either impotent fanaticism or else abject voluptuousness. Indian spirituality has been derided as ignorance, Chinese sobriety as stupidity, Japanese patriotism as the result of fatalism. It has been said that we are less sensible to pain and wounds on account of the callousness of our nervous organisation!

Why not amuse yourselves at our expense? Asia returns the compliment. There would be further food for merriment if you were to know all that we have imagined and written about you. All the glamour of the perspective is there, all the unconscious homage of wonder, all the silent resentment of the new and undefined. You have been loaded with virtues too refined to be envied, and accused of crimes too picturesque to be condemned. Our writers in the past—the wise men who knew—informed us that you had bushy tails somewhere hidden in your garments, and often dined off a fricassée of newborn babes! Nay, we had something worse against you: we used to think you the most impracticable people on the earth, for you were said to preach what you never practised.

Such misconceptions are fast vanishing amongst us. Commerce has forced the European tongues on many an Eastern port. Asiatic youths are flocking to Western colleges for the equipment of modern education. Our insight does not penetrate your culture deeply, but at least we are willing to learn. Some of my compatriots have adopted too much of your customs and too much of your etiquette, in the delusion that the acquisition of stiff collars and tall silk hats comprised the attainment of your civilisation. Pathetic and deplorable as such affectations are, they evince our willingness to approach the West on our knees. Unfortunately the Western attitude is unfavourable to the understanding of the East. The Christian missionary goes to impart, but not to receive. Your information is based on the meagre translations of our immense literature, if not on the unreliable anecdotes of passing travellers. It is rarely that the chivalrous pen of a Lafcadio Hearn or that of the author of "The Web of Indian Life" enlivens the Oriental darkness with the torch of our own sentiments.

Perhaps I betray my own ignorance of the Tea Cult by being so outspoken. Its very spirit of politeness exacts that you say what you are expected to say, and no more. But I am not to be a polite Teaist. So much harm has been done already by the mutual misunderstanding of the New World and the Old, that one need not apologise for contributing his tithe to the furtherance of a better understanding. The beginning of the twentieth century would have been spared the spectacle of sanguinary warfare if Russia had condescended to know Japan better. What dire consequences to humanity lie in the contemptuous ignoring of Eastern problems! European imperialism, which does not disdain to raise the absurd cry of the Yellow Peril, fails to realise that Asia may also awaken to the cruel sense of the White Disaster. You may laugh at us for having "too much tea," but may we not suspect that you of the West have "no tea" in your constitution?

Let us stop the continents from hurling epigrams at each other, and be sadder if not wiser by the mutual gain of half a hemisphere. We have developed along different lines, but there is no reason why one should not supplement the other. You have gained expansion at the cost of restlessness; we have created a harmony which is weak against aggression. Will you believe it?—the East is better off in some respects than the West!

Strangely enough humanity has so far met in the tea-cup. It is the only Asiatic ceremonial which commands universal esteem. The white man has scoffed at our religion and our morals, but has accepted the brown beverage without hesitation. The afternoon tea is now an important function in Western society. In the delicate clatter of trays and saucers, in the soft rustle of feminine hospitality, in the common catechism about cream and sugar, we know that the Worship of Tea is established beyond question. The philosophic resignation of the guest to the fate awaiting him in the dubious decoction proclaims that in this single instance the Oriental spirit reigns supreme.

The earliest record of tea in European writing is said to be found in the statement of an Arabian traveller, that after the year 879 the main sources of revenue in Canton were the duties on salt and tea. Marco Polo records the deposition of a Chinese minister of finance in 1285 for his arbitrary augmentation of the tea-taxes. It was at the period of the great discoveries that the European people began to know more about the extreme Orient. At the end of the sixteenth century the Hollanders brought the news that a pleasant drink was made in the East from the leaves of a bush. The travellers Giovanni Batista Ramusio (1559), L. Almeida (1576), Maffeno (1588), Tareira (1610), also mentioned tea. In the last-named year ships of the Dutch East India Company brought the first tea into Europe. It was known in France in 1636, and reached Russia in 1638. England welcomed it in 1650 and spoke of it as "That excellent and by all physicians approved China drink, called by the Chineans Tcha, and by other nations Tay, alias Tee."

Like all the good things of the world, the propaganda of Tea met with opposition. Heretics like Henry Saville (1678) denounced drinking it as a filthy custom. Jonas Hanway (Essay on Tea, 1756) said that men seemed to lose their stature and comeliness, women their beauty through the use of tea. Its cost at the start (about fifteen or sixteen shillings a pound) forbade popular consumption, and made it "regalia for high treatments and entertainments, presents being made thereof to princes and grandees." Yet in spite of such drawbacks tea-drinking spread with marvellous rapidity. The coffee-houses of London in the early half of the eighteenth century became, in fact, teahouses, the resort of wits like Addison and Steele, who beguiled themselves over their "dish of tea." The beverage soon became a necessary of life—a taxable matter. We are reminded in this connection what an important part it plays in modern history. Colonial America resigned herself to oppression until human endurance gave way before the heavy duties laid on Tea. American independence dates from the throwing of tea-chests into Boston harbour.

There is a subtle charm in the taste of tea which makes it irresistible and capable of idealisation. Western humourists were not slow to mingle the fragrance of their thought with its aroma. It has not the arrogance of wine, the self-consciousness of coffee, nor the simpering innocence of cocoa. Already in 1711, says the Spectator: "I would therefore in a particular manner recommend these my speculations to all well-regulated families that set apart an hour every morning for tea, bread and butter; and would earnestly advise them for their good to order this paper to be punctually served up and to be looked upon as a part of the tea-equipage." Samuel Johnson draws his own portrait as "a hardened and shameless tea-drinker, who for twenty years diluted his meals with only the infusion of the fascinating plant; who with tea amused the evening, with tea solaced the midnight, and with tea welcomed the morning."

Charles Lamb, a professed devotee, sounded the true note of Teaism when he wrote that the greatest pleasure he knew was to do a good action by stealth, and have it found out by accident. For Teaism is the art of concealing beauty that you may discover it, of suggesting what you dare not reveal. It is the noble secret of laughing at yourself, calmly yet thoroughly, and is thus humour itself,—the smile of philosophy. All genuine humourists may in this sense be called tea-philosophers,—Thackeray, for instance, and, of course, Shakespeare. The poets of the Decadence (when was not the world in decadence?), in their protests against materialism, have, to a certain extent, also opened the way to Teaism. Perhaps nowadays it is our demure contemplation of the Imperfect that the West and the East can meet in mutual consolation.

The Taoists relate that at the great beginning of the No-Beginning, Spirit and Matter met in mortal combat. At last the Yellow Emperor, the Sun of Heaven, triumphed over Shuhyung, the demon of darkness and earth. The Titan, in his death agony, struck his head against the solar vault and shivered the blue dome of jade into fragments. The stars lost their nests, the moon wandered aimlessly among the wild chasms of the night. In despair the Yellow Emperor sought far and wide for the repairer of the Heavens. He had not to search in vain. Out of the Eastern sea rose a queen, the divine Niuka, horn-crowned and dragon-tailed, resplendent in her armour of fire. She welded the five-coloured rainbow in her magic cauldron and rebuilt the Chinese sky. But it is also told that Niuka forgot to fill two tiny crevices in the blue firmament. Thus began the dualism of love—two souls rolling through space and never at rest until they join together to complete the universe. Everyone has to build anew his sky of hope and peace.

The heaven of modern humanity is indeed shattered in the Cyclopean struggle for wealth and power. The world is groping in the shadow of egotism and vulgarity. Knowledge is bought through a bad conscience, benevolence practised for the sake of utility. The East and West, like two dragons tossed in a sea of ferment, in vain strive to regain the jewel of life. We need a Niuka again to repair the grand devastation; we await the great Avatar. Meanwhile, let us have a sip of tea. The afternoon glow is brightening the bamboos, the fountains are bubbling with delight, the soughing of the pines is heard in our kettle. Let us dream of evanescence, and linger in the beautiful foolishness of things.

H. M. TOMLINSON

# Bed-Books and Night-Lights

The rain flashed across the midnight window with a myriad feet. There was a groan in outer darkness, the voice of all nameless dreads. The nervous candle-flame shuddered by my bedside. The groaning rose to a shriek, and the little flame jumped in a panic, and nearly left its white column. Out of the corners of the room swarmed the released shadows. Black specters danced in ecstasy over my bed. I love fresh air, but I cannot allow it to slay the shining and delicate body of my little friend the candle-flame, the comrade who ventures with me into the solitudes beyond midnight. I shut the window.

They talk of the candle-power of an electric bulb. What do they mean? It cannot have the faintest glimmer of the real power of my candle. It would be as right to express, in the same inverted and foolish comparison, the worth of "those delicate sisters, the Pleiades." That pinch of star dust, the Pleiades, exquisitely remote in deepest night, in the profound where light all but fails, has not the power of a sulphur match; yet, still apprehensive to the mind though tremulous on the limit of vision, and sometimes even vanishing, it brings into distinction those distant and difficult hints—hidden far behind all our verified thoughts—which we rarely properly view. I should like to know of any great are-lamp which could do that. So the star-like candle for me. No other light follows so intimately an author's most ghostly suggestion. We sit, the candle and I, in the midst of the shades we are conquering, and sometimes look up from the lucent page to contemplate the dark hosts of the enemy with a smile before they overwhelm us; as they will, of course. Like me, the candle is mortal; it will burn out.

As the bed-book itself should be a sort of night-light, to assist its illumination, coarse lamps are useless. They would douse the book. The light for such a book must accord with it. It must be, like the book, a limited, personal, mellow, and companionable glow; the solitary taper beside the only worshiper in a sanctuary. That is why nothing can compare with the intimacy of candle-light for a bed-book. It is a living heart, bright and warm in central night, burning for us alone, holding the gaunt and towering shadows at bay. There the monstrous specters stand in our midnight room, the advance guard of the darkness of the world, held off by our valiant little glim, but ready to flood instantly and founder us in original gloom.

The wind moans without; ancient evils are at large and wandering in torment. The rain shrieks across the window. For a moment, for just a moment, the sentinel candle is shaken, and burns blue with terror. The shadows leap out instantly. The little flame recovers, and merely looks at its foe the darkness, and back to its own place goes the old enemy of light and man. The candle for me, tiny, mortal, warm, and brave, a golden lily on a silver stem!

"Almost any book does for a bed-book," a woman once said to me. I nearly replied in a hurry that almost any woman would do for a wife; but that is not the way to bring people to conviction of sin. Her idea was that the bed-book is soporific, and for that reason she even advocated the reading of political speeches. That would be a dissolute act. Certainly you would go to sleep; but in what a frame of mind! You would enter into sleep with your eyes shut. It would be like dying, not only unshriven, but in the act of guilt.

What book shall it shine upon? Think of Plato, or Dante, or Tolstoy, or a Blue Book for such an occasion! I cannot. They will not do—they are no good to me. I am not writing about you. I know those men I have named are transcendent, the greater lights. But I am bound to confess at times they bore me. Though their feet are clay and on earth, just as ours, their stellar brows are sometimes dim in remote clouds. For my part, they are too big for bed-fellows. I cannot see myself, carrying my feeble and restricted glim, following (in pajamas) the statuesque figure of the Florentine where it stalks, aloof in its garb of austere pity, the sonorous deeps of Hades. Hades! Not for me; not after midnight! Let those go who like it.

As for the Russian, vast and disquieting, I refuse to leave all, including the blankets and the pillow, to follow him into the gelid tranquillity of the upper air, where even the colors are prismatic spicules of ice, to brood upon the erratic orbit of the poor mud-ball below called earth. I know it is my world also; but I cannot help that. It is too late, after a busy day, and at that hour, to begin overtime on fashioning a new and better planet out of cosmic dust. By breakfast-time, nothing useful would have been accomplished. We should all be where we were the night before. The job is far too long, once the pillow is nicely set.

For the truth is, there are times when we are too weary to remain attentive and thankful under the improving eye, kindly but severe, of the seers. There are times when we do not wish to be any better than we are. We do not wish to be elevated and improved. At midnight, away with such books! As for the literary pundits, the high priests of the Temple of Letters, it is interesting and helpful occasionally for an acolyte to swinge them a good hard one with an incense-burner, and cut and run, for a change, to something outside the rubrics. Midnight is the time when one can recall, with ribald delight, the names of all the Great Works which every gentleman ought to have read, but which some of us have not. For there is almost as much clotted nonsense written about literature as there is about theology.

There are few books which go with midnight, solitude, and a candle. It is much easier to say what does not please us then than what is exactly right. The book must be, anyhow, something benedictory by a sinning fellow-man. Cleverness would be repellent at such an hour. Cleverness, anyhow, is the level of mediocrity to-day; we are all too infernally clever. The first witty and perverse paradox blows out the candle. Only the sick in mind crave cleverness, as a morbid body turns to drink. The late candle throws its beams a great distance; and its rays make transparent much that seemed massy and important. The mind at rest beside that light, when the house is asleep, and the consequential affairs of the urgent world have diminished to their right proportions because we see them distantly from another and a more tranquil place in the heavens where duty, honor, witty arguments, controversial logic on great questions, appear such as will leave hardly a trace of fossil in the indurated mud which presently will cover them—the mind then certainly smiles at cleverness.

For though at that hour the body may be dog-tired, the mind is white and lucid, like that of a man from whom a fever has abated. It is bare of illusions. It has a sharp focus, small and starlike, as a clear and lonely flame left burning by the altar of a shrine from which all have gone but one. A book which approaches that light in the privacy of that place must come, as it were, with honest and open pages.

I like Heine then, though. His mockery of the

grave and great, in those sentences which are as brave as pennants in a breeze, is comfortable and sedative. One's own secret and awkward convictions, never expressed because not lawful and because it is hard to get words to bear them lightly, seem then to be heard aloud in the mild, easy, and confident diction of an immortal whose voice has the blitheness of one who has watched, amused and irreverent, the high gods in eager and secret debate on the best way to keep the gilt and trappings on the body of the evil they have created.

That first-rate explorer, Gulliver, is also fine in the light of the intimate candle. Have you read lately again his Voyage to the Houyhnhnms? Try it alone again in quiet. Swift knew all about our contemporary troubles. He has got it all down. Why was he called a misanthrope? Reading that last voyage of Gulliver in the select intimacy of midnight I am forced to wonder, not at Swift's hatred of mankind, not at his satire of his fellows, not at the strange and terrible nature of this genius who thought that much of us, but how it is that after such a wise and sorrowful revealing of the things we insist on doing, and our reasons for doing them, and what happens after we have done them, men do not change. It does seem impossible that society could remain unaltered, after the surprise its appearance should have caused it as it saw its face in that ruthless mirror. We point instead to the fact that Swift lost his mind in the end. Well, that is not a matter for surprise.

Such books, and France's "Isle of Penguins," are not disturbing as bed-books. They resolve one's agitated and outraged soul, relieving it with some free expression for the accusing and questioning thoughts engendered by the day's affairs. But they do not rest immediately to hand in the book-shelf by the bed. They depend on the kind of day one has had. Sterne is closer. One would rather be transported as far as possible from all the disturbances of earth's envelope of clouds, and "Tristram Shandy" is sure to be found in the sun.

But best of all books for midnight are travel books. Once I was lost every night for months with Doughty in the "Arabia Deserta." He is a craggy author. A long course of the ordinary facile stuff, such as one gets in the Press every day, thinking it is English, sends one thoughtless and headlong among the bitter herbs and stark boulders of Doughty's burning and spacious expanse; only to get bewildered, and the shins broken, and a great fatigue at first, in a strange land of fierce sun, hunger, glittering spar, ancient plutonic rock, and very Adam himself. But once you are acclimatized, and know the language—it takes time—there is no more London after dark, till, a wanderer returned from a forgotten land, you emerge from the interior of Arabia on the Red Sea coast again, feeling as though you had lost touch with the world you used to know. And if that doesn't mean good writing I know of no other test.

Because once there was a father whose habit it was to read with his boys nightly some chapters of the Bible—and cordially they hated that habit of his—I have that Book too; though I fear I have it for no reason that he, the rigid old faithful, would be pleased to hear about. He thought of the future when he read the Bible; I read it for the past. The familiar names, the familiar rhythm of its words, its wonderful well-remembered stories of things long past—like that of Esther, one of the best in English—the eloquent anger of the prophets for the people then who looked as though they were alive, but were really dead at heart, all is solace and home to me. And now I think of it, it is our home and solace that we want in a bed-book.

ROBERT LOUIS STEVENSON

**An Apology for Idlers**

"BOSWELL: *We grow weary when idle.*
"JOHNSON: *That is, sir, because others being
busy, we want company; but if we were idle,
there would be no growing weary; we should
all entertain one another.*"

Just now, when every one is bound, under
pain of a decree in absence convicting them of
*lèse*-respectability, to enter on some lucrative profession, and labour therein with something not
far short of enthusiasm, a cry from the opposite
party who are content when they have enough,
and like to look on and enjoy in the meanwhile,
savours a little of bravado and gasconade. And
yet this should not be. Idleness so called, which
does not consist in doing nothing, but in doing
a great deal not recognised in the dogmatic for-
mularies of the ruling class, has as good a right to

state its position as industry itself. It is admitted that the presence of people who refuse to enter in the great handicap race for sixpenny pieces, is at once an insult and a disenchantment for those who do. A fine fellow (as we see so many) takes his determination, votes for the sixpences, and in the emphatic Americanism, "goes for" them. And while such an one is ploughing distressfully up the road, it is not hard to understand his resentment, when he perceives cool persons in the meadows by the wayside, lying with a handkerchief over their ears and a glass at their elbow. Alexander is touched in a very delicate place by the disregard of Diogenes. Where was the glory of having taken Rome for these tumultuous barbarians, who poured into the Senate house, and found the Fathers sitting silent and unmoved by their success? It is a sore thing to have laboured along and sealed the arduous hilltops, and when all is done, find humanity indifferent to your achievement. Hence physicists condemn the unphysical; financiers have only a superficial toleration for those who know little of stocks; literary persons despise the unlettered; and people of all pursuits combine to disparage those who have none.

But though this is one difficulty of the subject,

it is not the greatest. You could not be put in prison for speaking against industry, but you can be sent to Coventry for speaking like a fool. The greatest difficulty with most subjects is to do them well; therefore, please to remember this is an apology. It is certain that much may be judiciously argued in favour of diligence; only there is something to be said against it, and that is what, on the present occasion, I have to say. To state one argument is not necessarily to be deaf to all others, and that a man has written a book of travels in Montenegro, is no reason why he should never have been to Richmond.

It is surely beyond a doubt that people should be a good deal idle in youth. For though here and there a Lord Macaulay may escape from school honours with all his wits about him, most boys pay so dear for their medals that they never afterwards have a shot in their locker, and begin the world bankrupt. And the same holds true during all the time a lad is educating himself, or suffering others to educate him. It must have been a very foolish old gentleman who addressed Johnson at Oxford in these words: "Young man, ply your book diligently now, and acquire a stock of knowledge; for when years come upon you, you will find that poring upon books will be but an irksome task." The old gentleman seems to have been unaware that many other things besides reading grow irksome, and not a few become impossible, by the time a man has to use spectacles and cannot walk without a stick. Books are good enough in their own way, but they are a mighty bloodless substitute for life. It seems a pity to sit, like the Lady of Shalott, peering into a mirror, with your back turned on all the bustle and glamour of reality. And if a man reads very hard, as the old anecdote reminds us, he will have little time for thoughts.

If you look back on your own education, I am sure it will not be the full, vivid, instructive hours of truantry that you regret; you would rather cancel some lack-lustre periods between sleep and waking in the class. For my own part, I have attended a good many lectures in my time. I still remember that the spinning of a top is a case of Kinetic Stability. I still remember that Emphyteusis is not a disease, nor Stillicide a crime. But though I would not willingly part with such scraps of science, I do not set the same store by them as by certain other odds and ends that I came by in the open street while I was playing truant. This is not the moment to dilate on that mighty place of education, which was the favourite school of

Dickens and of Balzac, and turns out yearly many inglorious masters in the Science of the Aspects of Life. Suffice it to say this: if a lad does not learn in the streets, it is because he has no faculty of learning. Nor is the truant always in the streets, for if he prefers, he may go out by the gardened suburbs into the country. He may pitch on some tuft of lilacs over a burn, and smoke innumerable pipes to the tune of the water on the stones. A bird will sing in the thicket. And there he may fall into a vein of kindly thought, and see things in a new perspective. Why, if this be not education, what is? We may conceive Mr. Worldly Wiseman accosting such an one, and the conversation that should thereupon ensue:—

"How, now, young fellow, what dost thou here?"

"Truly, sir, I take mine ease."

"Is not this the hour of the class? and should'st thou not be plying thy Book with diligence, to the end thou mayest obtain knowledge?"

"Nay, but thus also I follow after Learning, by your leave."

"Learning, quotha! After what fashion, I pray thee? Is it mathematics?"

"No, to be sure."

"Is it metaphysics?"

"Nor that."

"Is it some language!"

"Nay, it is no language."

"Is it a trade?"

"Nor a trade neither."

"Why, then, what is't?"

"Indeed, sir, as a time may soon come for me to go upon Pilgrimage, I am desirous to note what is commonly done by persons in my case, and where are the ugliest Sloughs and Thickets on the Road; as also, what manner of Staff is of the best service. Moreover, I lie here, by this water, to learn by root-of-heart a lesson which my master teaches me to call Peace, or Contentment."

Hereupon, Mr. Worldly Wiseman was much commoved with passion, and shaking his cane with a very threatful countenance, broke forth upon this wise: "Learning, quotha!" said he; "I would have all such rogues scourged by the Hangman!"

And so he would go his way, ruffling out his cravat with a crackle of starch, like a turkey when it spread its feathers.

Now this, of Mr. Wiseman, is the common opinion. A fact is not called a fact, but a piece of gossip, if it does not fall into one of your scholastic categories. An inquiry must be in some acknowledged direction, with a name to go by; or else you are not inquiring at all, only lounging; and the workhouse is too good for you. It is supposed that all knowledge is at the bottom of a well, or the far end of a telescope. Sainte-Beuve, as he grew older, came to regard all experience as a single great book, in which to study for a few years ere we go hence; and it seemed all one to him whether you should read in Chapter xx., which is the differential calculus, or in Chapter xxxix., which is hearing the band play in the gardens. As a matter of fact, an intelligent person, looking out of his eyes and hearkening in his ears, with a smile on his face all the time, will get more true education than many another in a life of heroic vigils. There is certainly some chill and arid knowledge to be found upon the summits of formal and laborious science; but it is all round about you, and for the trouble of looking, that you will acquire the warm and palpitating facts of life. While others are filling their memory with a lumber of words, one-half of which they will forget before the week be out, your truant may learn some really useful art: to play the fiddle, to know a good cigar, or to speak with ease and opportunity to all varieties of men. Many who have "plied their book diligently," and know all about some one branch or another of accepted lore, come out of the study with an ancient and owl-like demeanour, and prove dry, stockish, and dyspeptic in all the better and brighter parts of life. Many make a large fortune, who remain underbred and pathetically stupid to the last. And meantime there goes the idler, who began life along with them—by your leave, a different picture. He has had time to take care of his health and his spirits; he has been a great deal in the open air, which is the most salutary of all things for both body and mind; and if he has never read the great Book in very recondite places, he has dipped into it and skimmed it over to excellent purpose. Might not the student afford some Hebrew roots, and the business man some of his half-crowns, for a share of the idler's knowledge of life at large, and Art of Living? Nay, and the idler has another and more important quality than these. I mean his wisdom. He who has much looked on at the childish satisfaction of other people in their hobbies, will regard his own with only a very ironical indulgence. He will not be heard among the dogmatists. He will have a great and cool allowance for all sorts of people and opinions. If he finds no out-of-the-way truths, he will identify himself with no very burning falsehood. His way took him along a by-road, not much frequented, but very even and pleasant, which is called Commonplace Lane, and leads to the Belvedere of Commonsense. Thence he shall command an agreeable, if no very noble prospect; and while others behold the East and West, the Devil and the Sunrise, he will be contentedly aware of a sort of morning hour upon all sublunary things, with an army of shadows running speedily and in many different directions into the great daylight of Eternity. The shadows and the generations, the shrill doctors and the plangent wars, go by into ultimate silence and emptiness; but underneath all this, a man may see, out of the Belvedere windows, much green and peaceful landscape; many firelit parlours; good people laughing, drinking, and making love as they did before the Flood or the French Revolution; and the old shepherd telling his tale under the hawthorn.

Extreme *busyness*, whether at school or college, kirk or market, is a symptom of deficient vitality; and a faculty for idleness implies a catholic appetite and a strong sense of personal identity. There is a sort of dead-alive, hackneyed people about, who are scarcely conscious of living except in the exercise of some conventional occupation. Bring these fellows into the country, or set them aboard ship, and you will see how they pine for their desk or their study. They have no curiosity; they cannot give themselves over to random provocations; they do not take pleasure in the exercise of their faculties for its own sake; and unless Necessity lays about them with a stick, they will even stand still. It is no good speaking to such folk: they *cannot* be idle, their nature is not generous enough; and they pass those hours in a sort of coma, which are not dedicated to furious moiling in the gold-mill. When they do not require to go to the office, when they are not hungry and have no mind to drink, the whole breathing world is a blank to them. If they have to wait an hour or so for a train, they fall into a stupid trance with their eyes open. To see them, you would suppose there was nothing to look at and no one to speak with; you would imagine they were paralysed or alienated; and yet very possibly they are hard workers in their own way, and have good eyesight for a flaw in a deed or a turn of the market. They have been to school and college, but all the time they had their eye on the medal; they have gone about in the world and mixed with clever people, but all the time they were thinking of their own affairs. As if a man's soul were not too small to begin with, they have dwarfed and narrowed theirs by a life of all work and no play; until here they are at forty, with a listless attention, a mind vacant of all material of amusement, and not one thought to rub against another, while they wait for the train. Before he was breeched, he might have clambered on the boxes; when he was twenty, he would have stared at the girls; but now the pipe is smoked out, the snuffbox empty, and my gentleman sits bolt upright upon a bench, with lamentable eyes. This does not appeal to me as being Success in Life.

But it is not only the person himself who suffers from his busy habits, but his wife and children, his friends and relations, and down to the very people he sits with in a railway carriage or an omnibus. Perpetual devotion to what a man calls his business, is only to be sustained by perpetual neglect of many other things. And it is not by any means certain that a man's business is the most important thing he has to do. To an impartial estimate it will seem clear that many of the wisest, most virtuous, and most beneficent parts that are to be played upon the Theatre of Life are filled by gratuitous performers, and pass, among the world at large, as phases of idleness. For in that Theatre not only the walking gentlemen, singing chambermaids, and diligent fiddlers in the orchestra, but those who look on and clap their hands from the benches, do really play a part and fulfil important offices towards the general result. You are no doubt very dependent on the care of your lawyer and stockbroker, of the guards and signalmen who convey you rapidly from place to place, and the policemen who walk the streets for your protection; but is there not a thought of gratitude in your heart for certain other benefactors who set you smiling when they fall in your way, or season your dinner with good company? Colonel Newcome helped to lose his friend's money; Fred Bayham had an ugly trick of borrowing shirts; and yet they were better people to fall among than Mr. Barnes. And though Falstaff was neither sober nor very honest, I think I could name one or two long-faced Barabbases whom the world could better have done without. Hazlitt mentions that he was more sensible of obligation to Northcote, who had never done him anything he could call a service, than to his whole circle of ostentatious friends; for he thought a good companion emphatically the greatest benefactor. I know there are people in the world who cannot feel grateful unless the favour has been done them at the cost of pain and difficulty. But this is a churlish disposition. A man may send you six sheets of letter-paper covered with the most entertaining gossip, or you may pass half an hour pleasantly, perhaps profitably, over an article of his; do you think the service would be greater, if he had made the manuscript in his heart's blood, like a compact with the devil? Do you really fancy you should be more beholden to your correspondent, if he had been damning you all the while for your importunity? Pleasures are more beneficial than duties because, like the quality of mercy, they are not strained, and they are twice blest. There must always be two to a kiss, and there may be a score in a jest; but wherever there is an element of sacrifice, the favour is conferred with pain, and, among generous people, received with confusion. There is no duty we so much underrate as the duty of being happy. By being happy, we sow anonymous benefits upon the world, which remain unknown even to ourselves, or when they are disclosed, surprise nobody so much as the benefactor. The other day, a ragged, barefoot boy ran down the street after a marble, with so jolly an air that he set every one he passed into a good humour; one of these persons, who had been delivered from more than usually black thoughts, stopped the little fellow and gave him some money with this remark: "You see what sometimes comes of looking pleased." If he had looked pleased before, he had now to look both pleased and mystified. For my part, I justify this encouragement of smiling rather than tearful children; I do not wish to pay for tears anywhere but upon the stage; but I am prepared to deal largely in the opposite commodity. A happy man or woman is a better thing to find than a five-pound note. He or she is a radiating focus of good-will; and their entrance into a room is as though another candle had been lighted. We need not care whether they could prove the forty-seventh proposition; they do a better thing than that, they practically demonstrate the great Theorum of the liveableness of Life. Consequently, if a person cannot be happy without remaining idle, idle he should remain. It is a revolutionary precept; but thanks to hunger and the workhouse, one not easily to be abused; and within practical limits, it is one of the most incontestable truths in the whole Body of Morality. Look at one of your industrious fellows for a moment, I beseech you. He sows hurry and reaps indigestion; he puts a vast deal of activity out to interest, and receives a large measure of nervous derangement in return. Either he absents himself entirely from all fellowship, and lives a recluse in a garret, with carpet slippers and a leaden inkpot; or he comes among people swiftly and bitterly, in a contraction of his whole nervous system, to discharge some temper before he returns to work. I do not care how much or how well he works, this fellow is an evil feature in other people's lives. They would be happier if he were dead. They could easier do without his services in the Circumlocution Office, than they can tolerate his fractious spirits. He poisons life at the well-head. It is better to be beggared out of hand by a scapegrace nephew, than daily hag-ridden by a peevish uncle.

And what, in God's name, is all this pother about? For what cause do they embitter their own and other people's lives? That a man should publish three or thirty articles a year, that he should finish or not finish his great allegorical picture, are questions of little interest to the world. The ranks of life are full; and although a thousand fall, there are always some to go into the breach. When they told Joan of Arc she should be at home minding women's work, she answered there were plenty to spin and wash. And so, even with your own rare gifts! When nature is "so careless of the single life," why should we coddle ourselves into the fancy that our own is of exceptional importance? Suppose Shakespeare had been knocked on the head some dark night in Sir Thomas Lucy's preserves, the world would have wagged on better or worse, the pitcher gone to the well, the scythe to the corn, and the student to his book; and no one been any the wiser of the loss. There are not many works extant, if you look the alternative all over, which are worth the price of a pound of tobacco to a man of limited means. This is a sobering reflection for the proudest of our earthly vanities. Even a tobacconist may, upon consideration, find no great cause for personal vainglory in the phrase; for although tobacco is an admirable sedative, the qualities necessary for retailing it are neither rare nor precious in themselves. Alas and alas! you may take it how you will, but the services of no single individual are indispensable. Atlas was just a gentleman with a protracted nightmare! And yet you see merchants who go and labour themselves into a great fortune and thence into bankruptcy court; scribblers who keep scribbling at little articles until their temper is a cross to all who come about them, as though Pharaoh should set the Israelites to make a pin instead of a pyramid; and fine young men who work themselves into a decline, and are driven off in a hearse with white plumes upon it. Would you not suppose these persons had been whispered, by the Master of the Ceremonies, the promise of some momentous destiny? and that this lukewarm bullet on which they play their farces was the bull's-eye and centrepoint of all the universe? And yet it is not so. The ends for which they give away their priceless youth, for all they know, may be chimerical or hurtful; the glory and riches they expect may never come, or may find them indifferent; and they and the world they inhabit are so inconsiderable that the mind freezes at the thought.

ROSE MACAULAY

**Bed**

## 1. Getting into it

When I consider how, in a human creature's normal life, each day, however long, however short, however weary, however merry, circumstanced by whatever disconcerting, extravagant, or revolting chances of destiny, ends in getting into bed—when I consider this, I wonder why each day is not a happy, hopeful, and triumphant march towards this delicious goal; why, when the sun downs and the evening hours run on, our hearts do not lighten and sing in the sure and certain hope of this recumbent bliss. If it were a bliss less recurrent, more rare and strange, its exquisite luxury would surely seem a conception for the immortal gods, beyond any man's deserts. Even through the cold and sober definition given by the dictionary, comfort and anticipation warmly throb. "It consists for the most part of a sack or mattress of sufficient size, stuffed with something soft or springy, raised generally upon a 'bed-stead' or support, and covered with sheets, blankets, etc., for the purpose of warmth. The name is given both to the whole structure in its most elaborate form, and, as in 'feather-bed,' to the stuffed sack or mattress which constitutes its essential part. (A person is said to be *in bed*, when undressed and covered with the bedclothes)."

What delicious memories and hopes do the quiet words evoke! A sack or mattress of sufficient size, stuffed with something soft or springy, raised generally upon a bedstead or support, and covered with sheets, blankets, etc., for the purpose of warmth. Can well-being further go? Yes: for the purpose of even greater warmth, there may be a rubber bottle filled with hot water. Reflecting on, and still more, experiencing, this state of Olympian, of almost lascivious pleasure, how one pities Titania sleeping sometime of the night on her bank among thyme, oxlips, violets and snakes, her only coverlet the cast skins of these reptiles, which serve us not for sheets but for shoes. She was but a fairy queen, and knew nothing of our soft human elaborations of comfort. "Thou shalt lie in a bed stuffed with turtle's feathers; swoon in perfumed linen, like the fellow was smothered in roses."

> *And to your more bewitching, see, the proud*
> *Plumpe Bed beare up, and swelling like a*
> > *cloud . . .*
> *. . . Throw, throw*
> *Your selves into the mighty over-flow*
> *Of that white Pride, and Drowne*
> *The might, with you, in floods of Downe . . .*

That is better than the bank where the wild thyme grows; better, even, almost certainly, than the bed which Eve made out of flowers in the blissful nuptial bower, or than the roses that smothered the fellow. Not that down is necessary, or even desirable: a good hair mattress over box springs is more resilient, and as accordant to the frame as one can wish. The down can fill the pillows. The sheets are of smooth, fine cambric; not linen, which is heavier, colder, and less pliable, even when perfumed. Blankets should be according to season and temperature; it is well to have one or two in reserve, cast back over the bed's foot.

Climb, then, into this paradise, this epicurism

of pleasure, this pretty world of peace. Push up the pillows, that they support the head at an angle as you lie sideways, your book held in one hand, its edge resting on the pillow. On the bed-head is a bright light canopied by an orange shade; it illustrates the page with soft radiance, so that it shines out of the environing shadows like a good deed in a naughty world. You are reading, I would suggest, a novel; preferably a novel which excites you by its story, lightly titillating, but not furrowing, the surface of the brain. Not poetry; not history; not essays; not voyages; not biography, archaeology, dictionaries, nor that peculiar literature which publishers call belles-lettres. These are for day-time reading; they are not somnifacient; they stimulate the mind, the aesthetic and appreciative faculties, the inventive imagination; in brief, they wake you up. You will never, I maintain, get to sleep on Shakespeare, Milton, or Marvell, or Hakluyt, or Boswell, or Montaigne, or Burton's *Anatomy*, or Sir Thomas Browne, or Herodotus, or any poetry or prose that fundamentally excites you by its beauty, or any work that imparts knowledge. These will light a hundred candles in your brain, startling it to vivid life. A story, and more particularly a story which you have not read before, will hold your attention gently on the page, leading it on from event to event, drowsily pleased to be involved in such fine adventures, which yet demand no thought. Let the story amuse, thrill interest, delight, it matters not which; but let it not animate, stimulate or disturb, for sleep, that shy nightbird, must not be startled back as it hovers over you with drowsy wings, circling ever near and nearer, until its feathers brush your eyes, and the book dips suddenly in your hand. Lay it aside then; push out the light; the dark bed, like a gentle pool of water, receives you; you sink into its encompassing arms, floating down the wandering trail of a dream, as down some straying river that softly twists and slides through goblin lands, now dipping darkly into blind caves, now emerging, lit with the odd phosphorescent light of oneiric reason, unsearchable and dark to waking eyes.

But what a small mischance can mar this clinic joy, this opulent bed of pleasure. Adam and Eve doubtless encountered pricks and thorns and crumpled leaves in their roseate couch, though we are reassured as to the completely unentomologous condition of the bridal bower. And our passible frames may meet, in some untended mattress, with a lump. Or, in some alien dwelling, beneath the roof-tree of callous friends, with coverings cold as charity, blankets scant and thin. The eiderdown, if eiderdown there be, may glide and slide to the floor, like a French *duvet*. The hot-bottle may leak. Your head may face the window, and the curtains be of white casement, with a gap between to admit the dawn. The bird of dawning may sing all night long. A clock may tick, and be too large to be shut in the wardrobe. There may be a thin, transaudient wall, and a snorer beyond it. Or a snorer in your very bed, or even a somniloquent. Worst of all, worse than any other clinic grief, almost too profound a grief to be so much as glanced at in a survey of pleasures, it is conceivable that the light may only be extinguishable by the door. I believe, nay, I assert with confidence and deliberation, having clearly in mind all other bedroom woes—such as hard mattress, flock pillows, scant covering, intrusive dawn, coan bird-songs, disappointed or fatiguing Jove, companions lapped and chrysalised in robbed blankets and close-gripped sheets, and yet turning and ever turning still—I say with deliberation, that this is the shrewdest stroke of fortune, the harshest bedroom chance, a light only extinguishable by the door.

## 2. Not getting out of it

Infinite and interminable rivers of eloquence have run, singing and murmuring on this inexhaustible theme. It is probable that all has been said or sung on it that can be sung or said. Yet one is bound to contribute one's tributary, one's little stream of eloquence, to the flood which has flowed down the ages in praise of this great joy. The point is, once in the bed of pleasure, why get out of it? Humanity sees this point clearly every morning, yet, nearly every morning, obfuscates it, deserts the sheltering couch (where so much of the business of life might be transacted if we so chose, and at so much less cost of labour and distraction), and steps into the cold embattled world without.

How long wilt thou sleep, O sluggard? when wilt thou arise out of thy sleep? Yet a little sleep, a little slumber, a little folding of the hands to sleep . . . Go to the ant, thou sluggard; consider her ways and be wise . . .

Yes, but the ant's bed (even if the female ant does leave it as early in the morning as is here implied), is but a poor miserable resting-place compared with ours; the phrase "to seek repose on an ant-bed" has been used as a synonym of fantastic mischoice. We must not be surprised if ants rise betimes, instead of replying, as we do, to those who rouse them, "You have waked me too soon, I must slumber again." Do not praise the ant's ready exsuscitation, but pity rather that entomological barrenness of invention which has never furnished this hard-worked insect with a really comfortable bed. Not for the ant the drowsy exit from delicious dreams to world of soft down, box springs, and sheets that gentlier lie than tired eyelids upon tired eyes. Not for her (or him) the lively cup that disperses the somniatory clouds from the brain, the clean newspaper hot from the press, discreetly waiting to unfold its strange matutinal tale, the pile of letters, each throbbing with its little human message, each shut behind its enveloping protecting veil, which need not be torn asunder until, or unless, we choose—not these for the ant, waking on her stinging heap to another busy, bustling, onerous, formicarian day. Unhappy insect, motion-obsessed, for ever dragging, fetching, carrying, from one site to another, objects which are very well where they are, like those porters in Paris stations who can let nothing lie . . . such labours she can scarcely begin too late in the day. Consider the ant's ways and be wise indeed, for her labour is like unto ours;

we too are for ever dragging, fetching, carrying, changing, objects which are very well as they are . . . such labours we too can scarcely begin too late in the day. The advantage we have over the ant is that we know it; we have reason, she only instinct.

Lie back, then, among pillows and, gently yet firmly encouched, await the onslaught of the bellicose day, whose buffets jar less rudely those who take them lying down. Yield to the storm; venture not out into it, and it will pass.

> *Thou shalt have thy Caudles*
> *before thou dost arise:*
> *For churlishnesse breeds sicknesse*
> *and danger therin lies.*

Thus spoke a better lover than all those who have shouted to wake their ladies at dawn, calling them slug-a-beds, pigs in straw, bidding them rise and dress and come a-maying, asking them why should they sleep when they have slept enough (what a question!), and, worst of all, telling them that their breakfast stays until they are up—water-gruel, sugar-sops, brown ale, and toast. A kind lover or husband would bring all these to the bedroom; an intelligent one would be consuming them there himself. After this meal (unless quite incapacitated by its various ingredients), you may lie and reflect on all the occupations and works which man has pursued in bed; how Milton therein composed much of *Paradise Lost*; how Dido and her court feasted Æneas and his warriors, and after supper listened to his mournful travelogue, all reclining on their couches; how emperors and dictators have lain on beds while damsels danced before them and made music; how Sir John Suckling practised and perfected in bed that card-playing by which he lived; how Hobbes did mathematics, drawing lines on his thigh and on the sheets; how generals have planned victories and ordered attacks; how the Kings of France received their ministers in bed and dispensed affairs of state; how Lady Mary Wortley Montague received poets, and Prime Ministers the news of victories; how men are born in bed, and frequently die there; how Samuel Pepys lay late with great pleasure, and Samuel Johnson lay all his life until noon or until two, purposing to rise at eight and telling young men that nobody who did not rise early would ever come to good. Indeed, so much of the world's business has been performed in bed, that even to begin to consider it will be a morning's work. Rise early and bed late, says a foolish old adage, but does not explain why you will be better out of bed than in. A thing too often forgotten is that, once you are out of it, you or someone else will have to make it. There was a certain man named Æneas who had kept his bed eight years, whom St. Peter bade arise, and added that he was to make his bed. Æneas arose, and, we suppose, made his bed; but, after eight years of lying in it, this daily rising and making it must have seemed very strange, and we are not told how long it lasted.

Indeed, more should be done in bed than is (even more). We spend too many of these precious clinic hours in blind stupor, tenebrizing it like polar bears in winter. Going to bed is a nocturnal pleasure; but not getting out of it is a journal one, to be enjoyed with all the innocent ardours and relish of the day. Slug then in sloth, and languish in delights, while the day breaks and shadows flee away.

But the luxury of pleasure is marred, as time creeps on, by a bitter foreknowledge born of experience. Sooner or later some one of those who are under your roof, unless you have your roof all day to yourself, will enquire if you are ill, and, if you are well, at what hour you are proposing to rise. Why, in the name of all the great bed-lovers, should I be ill because I prefer to remain in so charming a refuge as my bed? Did Milton's daughters ask him if he was ill when he preferred to dictate from his bed? Was Dr. Johnson ill? Were the French Kings? No, I am not ill; I am merely philoclinic . . . that is my answer, if I can but make it to her who arrives to clean my flat . . .

AGNES REPPLIER

**Leisure**

*"Zounds! how has he the leisure to be sick?"*

A visitor strolling through the noble woods of Ferney complimented Voltaire on the splendid growth of his trees. "Ay," replied the great wit, half in scorn and half, perhaps, in envy, "they have nothing else to do;" and walked on, deigning no further word of approbation.

Has it been more than a hundred years since this distinctly modern sentiment was uttered,— more than a hundred years since the spreading chestnut boughs bent kindly over the lean, strenuous, caustic, disappointed man of genius who always had so much to do, and who found in the doing of it a mingled bliss and bitterness that scorched him like fever pain? How is it that, while Dr. Johnson's sledge-hammer repartees sound like the sonorous echoes of a past age, Voltaire's remarks always appear to have been spoken the day before yesterday? They are the kind of witticisms which we do not say for ourselves, simply because we are not witty; but they illustrate with biting accuracy the spirit of restlessness, of disquiet, of intellectual vanity and keen contention which is the brand of our vehement and overzealous generation.

"The Gospel of Work"—that is the phrase woven insistently into every homily, every appeal made to the conscience or the intelligence of a people who are now straining their youthful energy to its utmost speed. "Blessed be Drudgery!"—that is the text deliberately chosen for a discourse which has enjoyed such amazing popularity that sixty thousand printed copies have been found all inadequate to supply the ravenous demand. Readers of Dickens—if any one has the time to read Dickens nowadays—may remember Miss Monflather's inspired amendment of that familiar poem concerning the Busy Bee:—

*"In work, work, work. In work alway,*
*Let my first years be past."*

And when our first years *are* past, the same programme is considered adequate and satisfactory to the end. "A whole lifetime of horrid industry,"—to quote Mr. Bagehot's uninspired words,—this is the prize dangled alluringly before our tired eyes; and if we are disposed to look askance upon the booty, then vanity is subtly pricked to give zest to faltering resolution. "Our virtues would be proud if our faults whipped them not;" they would be laggards in the field if our faults did not sometimes spur them to action. It is the pæan of self-glorification that wells up perpetually from press and pulpit, from public orators, and from what is courteously called literature, that keeps our courage screwed to the sticking place, and veils the occasional bareness of the result with a charitable vesture of self-delusion.

Work is good. No one seriously doubts this truth. Adam may have doubted it when he first took spade in hand, and Eve when she scoured her first pots and kettles; but in the course of a few thousand years we have learned to know and value this honest, troublesome, faithful, and extremely exacting friend. But work is not the only good thing in the world; it is not a fetich to be adored: neither is it to be judged, like a sum in addition, by its outward and immediate results. The god of labor does not abide exclusively in the rolling-mill, the law courts, or the cornfield. He has a twin sister whose name is leisure, and in her society he lingers now and then to the lasting gain of both.

Sainte-Beuve, writing of Mme. de Sévigné and her time, says that we, "with our habits of positive occupation, can scarcely form a just conception of that life of leisure and chit-chat." "Conversations were infinite," admits Mme. de Sévigné herself, recalling the long summer afternoons when she and her guests walked in the charming woods of Les Rochers until the shadows of twilight fell. The whole duty of life seemed to be concentrated in the pleasant task of entertaining your friends when they were with you, or writing them admirable letters when they were absent. Occasionally there came, even to this tranquil and finely poised French woman, a haunting consciousness that there might be other and harder work for human hands to do. "Nothing is accomplished day by day," she writes, doubtfully; "and life is made up of days, and we grow old and die." This troubled her a little, when she was all the while doing work that was to last for generations, work that was to give pleasure to men and women whose great-grandfathers were then unborn. Not that we have the time now to read Mme. de Sévigné!

Why, there are big volumes of these delightful letters, and who can afford to read big volumes of anything, merely for the sake of the enjoyment to be extracted therefrom? It was all very well for Sainte-Beuve to say "Lisons tout Mme. de Sévigné," when the question arose how should some long idle days in a country-house be profitably employed. It was all very well for Sainte-Beuve to plead, with touching confidence in the intellectual pastimes of his contemporaries, "Let us treat Mme. de Sévigné as we treat Clarissa Harlowe, when we have a fortnight of leisure and rainy weather in the country." A fortnight of leisure and rainy weather in the country! The words would be antiquated even for Dr. Johnson. Rain may fall or rain may cease, but leisure comes not so lightly to our calling. Nay, Sainte-Beuve's wistful amazement at the polished and cultivated inactivity which alone could produce such a correspondence as Mme. de Sévigné's is not greater than our wistful amazement at the critic's conception of possible idleness in bad weather. In one respect at least we follow his good counsel. We do treat Mme. de Sévigné precisely as we treat Clarissa Harlowe; that is, we leave them both severely alone, as being utterly beyond the reach of what we are pleased to call our time.

And what of the leisure of Montaigne, who, taking his life in his two hands, disposed of it as he thought fit, with no restless self-accusations on the score of indolence. In the world and of the world, yet always able to meet and greet the happy solitude of Gascony; toiling with no thought of toil, but rather "to entertain my spirit as it best pleased," this man wrought out of time a coin which passes current over the reading world. And what of Horace, who enjoyed an industrious idleness, the bare description of which sets our hearts aching with desire! "The picture which Horace draws of himself in his country home," says an envious English critic, "affords us a delightful glimpse of such literary leisure as is only possible in the golden days of good Haroun-Al-Raschid. Horace goes to bed and gets up when he likes; there is no one to drag him down to the law courts the first thing in the morning, to remind him of an important engagement with his brother scribes, to solicit his interest with Mæcenas, or to tease him about public affairs and the latest news from abroad. He can bury himself in his Greek authors, or ramble through the woody glens which lie at the foot of Mount Ustica, without a thought of business or a feeling that he ought to be otherwise engaged."

"Swim smoothly in the stream of thy nature, and live but one man," counsels Sir Thomas Browne; and it may be this gentle current will bear us as bravely through life as if we buffeted our strength away in the restless ocean of endeavor.

Leisure has a value of its own. It is not a mere handmaid of labor; it is something we should know how to cultivate, to use, and to enjoy. It has a distinct and honorable place wherever nations are released from the pressure of their first rude needs, their first homely toil, and rise to happier levels of grace and intellectual repose. "Civilization, in its final outcome," says the keen young author of "The Chevalier of Pensieri-Vani," "is heavily in the debt of leisure; and the success of any society worth considering is to be estimated largely by the use to which its *fortunati* put their spare moments." Here is a sentiment so relentlessly true that nobody wants to believe it. We prefer uttering agreeable platitudes concerning the blessedness of drudgery and the iniquity of eating bread earned by another's hands. Yet the creation of an artistic and intellectual atmosphere in which workers can work, the expansion of a noble sympathy with all that is finest and most beautiful, the jealous guardianship of whatever makes the glory and distinction of a nation; this is achievement enough for the *fortunati* of any land, and this is the debt they owe. It can hardly be denied that the lack of scholarship—of classical scholarship especially—at our universities is due primarily to the labor-worship which is the prevalent superstition of our day, and which, like all superstitions, has gradually degraded its god into an idol, and lost sight of the higher powers and attributes beyond. The student who is pleased to think a knowledge of German "more useful" than a knowledge of Greek; the parent who deliberately declares that his boys have "no time to waste" over Homer; the man who closes the doors of his mind to everything that does not bear directly on mathematics, or chemistry, or engineering, or whatever he calls "work;" all these plead in excuse the exigencies of life, the absolute and imperative necessity of labor.

It would appear, then, that we have no *fortunati*, that we are not yet rich enough to afford the greatest of all luxuries—leisure to cultivate and enjoy "the best that has been known and thought in the world." This is a pity, because there seems to be money in plenty for so many less valuable things. The yearly taxes of the United States sound to innocent ears like the fabled wealth of the Orient; the yearly expenditures of the people are on no rigid scale; yet we are too poor to harbor the priceless literature of the past because it is not a paying investment, because it will not put bread in our mouths nor clothes on our shivering nakedness. "Poverty is a most odious calling," sighed Burton many years ago, and we have good cause to echo his lament. Until we are able to believe, with that enthusiastic Greek scholar, Mr. Butcher, that "intellectual training is an end in itself, and not a mere preparation for a trade or a profession;" until we begin to understand that there is a leisure which does not mean an easy sauntering through life, but a special form of activity, employing all our faculties, and training us to the adequate reception of whatever is most valuable in literature and art; until we learn to estimate the fruits of self-culture at their proper worth, we are still far from reaping the harvest of three centuries of toil and struggle; we are still as remote as ever from the serenity of intellectual accomplishment.

There is a strange pleasure in work wedded to leisure, in work which has grown beautiful because its rude necessities are softened and humanized by sentiment and the subtle grace of association. A little paragraph from the journal of Eugénie de Guérin illustrates with charming simplicity the gilding of common toil by the delicate touch of a cultivated and sympathetic intelligence:—

"A day spent in spreading out a large wash leaves little to say, and yet it is rather pretty, too, to lay the white linen on the grass, or to see it float on lines. One may fancy one's self Homer's Nausicaa, or one of those Biblical princesses who washed their brothers' tunics. We have a basin at Moulinasse that you have never seen, sufficiently large, and full to the brim of water. It embellishes the hollow, and attracts the birds who like a cool place to sing in."

In the same spirit, Maurice de Guérin confesses frankly the pleasure he takes in gathering fagots for the winter fire, "that little task of the woodcutter which brings us close to nature," and which was also a favorite occupation of M. de Lamennais. The fagot gathering, indeed, can hardly be said to have assumed the proportions of real toil; it was rather a pastime where play was thinly disguised by a pretty semblance of drudgery. "Idleness," admits de Guérin, *but idleness full of thought, and alive to every impression.* Eugénie's labors, however, had other aspects and bore different fruit. There is nothing intrinsically charming in stitching seams, hanging out clothes, or scorching one's fingers over a kitchen fire; yet every page in the journal of this nobly born French girl reveals to us the nearness of work, work made sacred by the prompt fulfillment of visible duties, and—what is more rare—made beautiful by that distinction of mind which was the result of alternating hours of finely cultivated leisure. A very ordinary and estimable young woman might have spread her wash upon the grass with honest pride at the whiteness of her linen; but it needed the solitude of Le Cayla, the few books, well read and well worth reading, the life of patriarchal simplicity, and the habit of sustained and delicate thought, to awaken in the worker's mind the graceful association of ideas,—the pretty picture of Nausicaa and her maidens cleansing their finely woven webs in the cool, rippling tide.

For it is self-culture that warms the chilly earth wherein no good seed can mature; it is self-culture that distinguishes between the work which has inherent and lasting value and the work which represents conscientious activity and no more. And for the training of one's self, leisure is requisite; leisure and that rare modesty which turns a man's thoughts back to his own shortcomings and requirements, and extinguishes in him the burning desire to enlighten his fellow-beings. "We might make ourselves spiritual by detaching ourselves from action, and become perfect by the rejection of energy," says Mr. Oscar Wilde, who delights in scandalizing his patient readers, and who lapses unconsciously into something resembling animation over the wrongs inflicted by the solemn preceptors of mankind. The notion that it is worth while to learn a thing only if you intend to impart it to others is widespread and exceedingly popular. I have myself heard an excellent and anxious aunt say to her young niece, then working hard at college, "But, my dear, why do you give so much of your time to Greek? You don't expect to teach it, do you?"—as if there were no other use to be gained, no other pleasure to be won from that noble language, in which lies hidden the hoarded treasure of centuries. To study Greek in order to read and enjoy it, and thereby make life better worth the living, is a possibility that seldom enters the practical modern mind.

Yet this restless desire to give out information, like alms, is at best a questionable bounty; this determination to share one's wisdom with one's unwilling fellow-creatures is a noble impulse provocative of general discontent. When Southey, writing to James Murray about a dialogue which he proposes to publish in the "Quarterly," says, with characteristic complacency; "I have very little doubt that it will excite considerable attention, and lead many persons into a wholesome train of thought," we feel at once how absolutely familiar is the sentiment, and how absolutely hopeless is literature approached in this spirit. The same principle, working under different conditions to-day, entangles us in a network of lectures, which have become the chosen field for every educational novelty, and the diversion of the mentally unemployed.

Charles Lamb has recorded distinctly his veneration for the old-fashioned schoolmaster who taught his Greek and Latin in leisurely fashion day after day, with no thought wasted upon more superficial or practical acquirements, and who "came to his task as to a sport." He has made equally plain his aversion for the new-fangled pedagogue—new in his time, at least—who could not "relish a beggar or a gypsy" without seeking to collect or to impart some statistical information on the subject. A gentleman of this calibre, his fellow-traveler in a coach, once asked him if he had ever made "any calculation as to the value of the rental of all the retail shops in

London?" and the magnitude of the question so overwhelmed Lamb that he could not even stammer out a confession of his ignorance. "To go preach to the first passer-by, to become tutor to the ignorance of the first thing I meet, is a task I abhor," observes Montaigne, who must certainly have been the most acceptable companion of his day.

Dr. Johnson, too, had scant sympathy with insistent and arrogant industry. He could work hard enough when circumstances demanded it; but he "always felt an inclination to do nothing," and not infrequently gratified his desires. "No man, sir, is obliged to do as much as he can. A man should have part of his life to himself," was the good doctor's soundly heterodox view, advanced upon many occasions. He hated to hear people boast of their assiduity, and nipped such vain pretensions in the bud with frosty scorn. When he and Boswell journeyed together in the Harwich stage-coach, a "fat, elderly gentlewoman," who had been talking freely of her own affairs, wound up by saying that she never permitted any of her children to be for a moment idle. "I wish, madam," said Dr. Johnson testily, "that you would educate me too, for I have been an idle fellow all my life." "I am sure, sir," protested the woman with dismayed politeness, "you have not been idle." "Madam," was the retort, "it is true! And that gentleman there"—pointing to poor young Boswell—"has been idle also. He was idle in Edinburgh. His father sent him to Glasgow, where he continued to be idle. He came to London, where he has been very idle. And now he is going to Utrecht, where he will be as idle as ever."

That there was a background of truth in these spirited assertions we have every reason to be grateful. Dr. Johnson's value to-day does not depend on the number of essays, or reviews, or dedications he wrote in a year,—some years he wrote nothing,—but on his own sturdy and splendid personality; "the real primate, the soul's teacher of all England," says Carlyle; a great embodiment of uncompromising goodness and sense. Every generation needs such a man, not to compile dictionaries, but to preserve the balance of sanity, and few generations are blest enough to possess him. As for Boswell, he might have toiled in the law courts until he was gray without benefiting or amusing anybody. It was in the nights he spent drinking port wine at the Mitre, and in the days he spent trotting, like a terrier, at his master's heels, that the seed was sown which was to give the world a masterpiece of literature, the most delightful biography that has ever enriched mankind. It is to leisure that we owe the "Life of Johnson," and a heavy debt we must, in all integrity, acknowledge it to be.

Mr. Shortreed said truly of Sir Walter Scott that he was "making himself in the busy, idle pleasures of his youth;" in those long rambles by hill and dale, those whimsical adventures in farmhouses, those merry, purposeless journeys in which the eager lad tasted the flavor of life. At home such unauthorized amusements were regarded with emphatic disapprobation. "I greatly doubt, sir," said his father to him one day, "that you were born for nae better than a gangrel scrape-gut!" and one half pities the grave clerk to the Signet, whose own life had been so decorously dull, and who regarded with affectionate solicitude his lovable and incomprehensible son. In later years Sir Walter recognized keenly that his wasted school hours entailed on him a lasting loss, a loss he was determined his sons should never know. It is to be forever regretted that "the most Homeric of modern men could not read Homer." But every day he stole from the town to give to the country, every hour he stole from law to give to literature, every minute he stole from work to give to pleasure, counted in the end as gain. It is in his pleasures that a man really lives, it is from his leisure that he constructs the true fabric of self. Perhaps Charles Lamb's fellow clerks thought that because his days were spent at a desk in the East India House, his life was spent there too. His life was far remote from that routine of labor; built up of golden moments of respite, enriched with joys, chastened by sorrows, vivified by impulses that had no filiation with his daily toil. "For the time that a man may call his own," he writes to Wordsworth, "that is his life." The Lamb who worked in the India House, and who had "no skill in figures," has passed away, and is to-day but a shadow and a name. The Lamb of the "Essays" and the "Letters" lives for us now, and adds each year his generous share to the innocent gayety of the world. This is the Lamb who said, "Riches are chiefly good because they give us time," and who sighed for a little son that he might christen him Nothing-to-do, and permit him to do nothing.

JEROME K. JEROME

# On Being Idle

Now this is a subject on which I flatter myself I really am *au fait*. The gentleman who, when I was young, bathed me at wisdom's font for nine guineas a term—no extras—used to say he never knew a boy who could do less work in more time; and I remember my poor grandmother once incidentally observing, in the course of an instruction upon the use of the prayer-book, that it was highly improbable that I should ever do much that I ought to do, but that she felt convinced, beyond a doubt, that I should leave undone pretty well everything that I ought to do.

I am afraid I have somewhat belied half the dear old lady's prophecy. Heaven help me! I have done a good many things that I ought not to have done, in spite of my laziness. But I have fully confirmed the accuracy of her judgment so far as neglecting much that I ought not to have neglected is concerned. Idling always has been my strong point. I take no credit to myself in the matter—it is a gift. Few possess it. There are plenty of lazy people and plenty of slow-coaches, but a genuine idler is a rarity. He is not a man who slouches about with his hands in his pockets. On the contrary, his most startling characteristic is that he is always intensely busy.

It is impossible to enjoy idling thoroughly unless one has plenty of work to do. There is no fun in doing nothing when you have nothing to do. Wasting time is merely an occupation then, and a most exhausting one. Idleness, like kisses, to be sweet must be stolen.

Many years ago, when I was a young man, I was taken very ill—I never could see myself that much was the matter with me, except that I had a beastly cold. But I suppose it was something very serious, for the doctor said that I ought to have come to him a month before, and that if it (whatever it was) had gone on for another week he would not have answered for the consequences. It is an extraordinary thing, but I never knew a doctor called into any case yet, but what it transpired that another day's delay would have rendered cure hopeless. Our medical guide, philosopher, and friend is like the hero in a melo-drama, he always comes upon the scene just, and only just, in the nick of time. It is Providence, that is what it is.

Well, as I was saying, I was very ill, and was ordered to Buxton for a month, with strict injunctions to do nothing whatever all the while that I was there. "Rest is what you require," said the doctor, "perfect rest."

It seemed a delightful prospect. "This man evidently understands my complaint," said I, and I pictured to myself a glorious time—a four weeks' *dolce far niente* with a dash of illness in it. Not too much illness, but just illness enough—just sufficient to give it the flavor of suffering, and make it poetical. I should get up late, sip chocolate, and have my breakfast in slippers and a dressing-gown. I should lie out in the garden in a hammock, and read sentimental novels with a melancholy ending, until the book would fall from my listless hand, and I should recline there, dreamily gazing into the deep blue of the firmament, watching the fleecy clouds floating like white-sailed ships across its depths, and listening to the joyous song of the birds, and the low rustling of the trees. Or, when I became too weak to go out-of-doors, I should sit propped up with pillows, at the open window of the ground-floor front, and look wasted and interesting, so that all the pretty girls would sigh as they passed by.

And, twice a day, I should go down in a Bath chair to the Colonnade, to drink the waters. Oh, those waters! I knew nothing about them then, and was rather taken with the idea. "Drinking the waters" sounded fashionable and Queen Anneified, and I thought I should like them. But, ugh! after the first three or four mornings! Sam Weller's description of them, as "having a taste of warm flat-irons," conveys only a faint idea of their hideous nauseousness. If anything could make a sick man get well quickly, it would be the knowledge that he must drink a glassful of them every day until he had recovered. I drank them neat for six consecutive days, and they nearly killed me; but, after them, I adopted the plan of taking a stiff glass of brandy and water immediately on the top of them, and found much relief thereby. I have been informed since, by various eminent medical gentlemen, that the alcohol must have entirely counteracted the effects of the chalybeate properties contained in the water. I am glad I was lucky enough to hit upon the right thing.

But "drinking the waters" was only a small portion of the torture I experienced during that memorable month, a month which was, without exception, the most miserable I have ever spent. During the best part of it, I religiously followed the doctor's mandate, and did nothing whatever, except moon about the house and garden, and go out for two hours a day in a Bath chair. That did break the monotony to a certain extent. There is more excitement about Bath-chairing—especially if you are not used to the exhilarating exercise—than might appear to the casual observer. A sense of danger, such as a mere outsider might not understand, is ever present to the mind of the occupant. He feels convinced every minute that the whole concern is going over, a conviction which becomes especially lively whenever a ditch or a stretch of newly macadamized road comes in sight. Every vehicle that passes he expects is going to run into him; and he never finds himself ascending or descending a hill without immediately beginning to speculate upon his chances, supposing—as seems extremely probable—that the weak-kneed controller of his destiny should let go.

But even this diversion failed to enliven after a while, and the *ennui* became perfectly unbearable. I felt my mind giving way under it. It is not a strong mind, and I thought it would be unwise to tax it too far. So somewhere about the twentieth morning, I got up early, had a good breakfast, and walked straight off to Hayfield, at the foot of the Kinder Scout—a pleasant, busy, little town, reached through a lovely valley, and with two sweetly pretty women in it. At least they were sweetly pretty then; one passed me on the bridge, and, I think, smiled; and the other was standing at an open door, making an unremunerative investment of kisses upon a red-faced baby. But it is years ago, and I dare say they have both grown stout and snappish since that time. Coming back, I saw an old man breaking stones, and it roused such strong longing in me to use my arms that I offered him a drink to let me take his place. He was a kindly old man, and he humored me. I went for those stones with the accumulated energy of three weeks, and did more work in half an hour than he had done all day. But it did not make him jealous.

Having taken the plunge, I went further and further into dissipation, going out for a long walk every morning, listening to the band in the pavilion every evening. But the days still passed slowly notwithstanding, and I was heartily glad when the last one came, and I was being whirled away from gouty, consumptive Buxton to London with its stern work and life. I looked out of the carriage as we rushed through Hendon in the evening. The lurid glare overhanging the mighty city seemed to warm my heart, and when, later on, my cab rattled out of St. Pancras's Station, the old familiar roar that came swelling up around me sounded the sweetest music I had heard for many a long day.

I certainly did not enjoy that month's idling. I like idling when I ought not to be idling; not when it is the only thing I have to do. That is my pig-headed nature. The time when I like best to stand with my back to the fire, calculating how much I owe, is when my desk is heaped highest with letters that must be answered by the next post. When I like to dawdle longest over my dinner is when I have a heavy evening's work before me. And if, for some urgent reason, I ought to be up particularly early in the morning, it is then, more than any other time, that I love to lie an extra half hour in bed.

Ah! how delicious it is to turn over and go to sleep again: "just for five minutes!" Is there any human being, I wonder, besides the hero of a Sunday-school "tale for boys," who ever gets up willingly? There are some men to whom getting up at the proper time is an utter impossibility. If eight o'clock happens to be the time that they should turn out, then they lie till half-past. If circumstances change, and half-past eight becomes early enough for them, then it is nine before they can rise; they are like the statesman of whom it was said that he was always punctually half an hour late. They try all manner of schemes. They buy alarm clocks (artful contrivances, they go off at the wrong time, and alarm the wrong people). They tell Sarah Jane to knock at the door and call them, and Sarah Jane does knock at the door, and does call them, and they grunt back "Awri," and then go comfortably to sleep again. I knew one man who would actually get out, and have a cold bath; and even that was of no use, for, afterward, he would jump into bed again to warm himself.

I think myself that I could keep out of bed all right, if I once got out. It is the wrenching away of the head from the pillow that I find so hard, and no amount of overnight determination makes it easier. I say to myself, after having wasted the whole evening, "Well, I won't do any more work to-night; I'll get up early to-morrow morning;" and I am thoroughly resolved to do so—then. In the morning, however, I feel less enthusiastic about the idea, and reflect that it would have been much better if I had stopped up last night. And then there is the trouble of dressing, and the more one thinks about that, the more one wants to put it off.

It is a strange thing this bed, this mimic grave, where we stretch our tired limbs, and sink away so quietly into the silence and rest. "Oh, bed, oh, bed, delicious bed, that heaven on earth to the weary head," as sung poor Hood, you are a kind old nurse to us fretful boys and girls. Clever and foolish, naughty and good, you take us all in your motherly lap, and hush our way-ward crying. The strong man full of care—the sick man full of pain—the little maiden, sobbing for her faithless lover—like children, we lay our aching heads on your white bosom, and you gently soothe us off to by-by.

Our trouble is sore indeed when you turn away and will not comfort us. How long the dawn seems coming, when we can not sleep! Oh! those hideous nights, when we toss and turn in fever and pain, when we lie, like living men among the dead, staring out into the dark hours that drift so slowly between us and the light. And oh! those still more hideous nights, when we sit by another in pain, when the low fire startles us every now and then with a fallen cinder, and the tick of the clock seems a hammer, beating out the life that we are watching.

But enough of beds and bedrooms. I have kept to them too long, even for an idle fellow. Let us come out, and have a smoke. That wastes time just as well, and does not look so bad. Tobacco has been a blessing to us idlers. What the civil-service clerks before Sir Wolter's time found to occupy their minds with, it is hard to imagine. I attribute the quarrelsome nature of the Middle Ages young men entirely to the want of the soothing weed. They had no work to do, and could not smoke, and the consequence was they were forever fighting and rowing. If, by any extraordinary chance, there was no war going, then they got up a deadly family feud with the next-door neighbor, and if, in spite of this, they still had a few spare moments on their hands, they occupied them with discussions as to whose sweetheart was the best looking, the arguments employed on both sides being battle-axes, clubs, etc. Questions of taste were soon decided in those days. When a twelfth century youth fell in love, he did not take three paces backward, gaze into her eyes, and tell her she was too beautiful to live. He said he would step outside and see about it. And if, when he got out, he met a man and broke his head—the other man's head, I mean—then that proved that his—the first fellow's—girl was a pretty girl. But if the other fellow broke *his* head—not his own, you know, but the other fellow's—the other fellow to the second fellow, that is, because of course the other fellow would only be the other fellow to him, not the first fellow, who—well, if he broke his head, then *his* girl—not the other fellow's, but the fellow who *was* the—Look here, if A broke B's head, then A's girl was a pretty girl; but if B broke A's head, then A's girl wasn't a pretty girl, but B's girl was. That was their method of conducting art criticism.

Nowadays we light a pipe, and let the girls fight it out among themselves.

They do it very well. They are getting to do all our work. They are doctors, and barristers, and artists. They manage theatres, and promote swindles, and edit newspapers. I am looking forward to the time when we men shall have nothing to do but lie in bed till twelve, read two novels a day, have nice little five-o'clock teas all to ourselves, and tax our brains with nothing more trying than discussions upon the latest patterns in trousers, and arguments as to what Mr. Jones's coat was made of, and whether it fitted him. It is a glorious prospect—for idle fellows.

# Peace
# in the
# World

VIRGINIA WOOLF

# Thoughts on Peace
in an Air Raid

The Germans were over this house last night and the night before that. Here they are again. It is a queer experience, lying in the dark and listening to the zoom of a hornet which may at any moment sting you to death. It is a sound that interrupts cool and consecutive thinking about peace. Yet it is a sound—far more than prayers and anthems—that should compel one to think about peace. Unless we can think peace into existence we—not this one body in this one bed but millions of bodies yet to be born—will lie in the same darkness and hear the same death rattle overhead. Let us think what we can do to create the only efficient air-raid shelter while the guns on the hill go pop pop pop and the searchlights finger the clouds and now and then, sometimes close at hand, sometimes far away, a bomb drops.

Up there in the sky young Englishmen and young German men are fighting each other. The defenders are men, the attackers are men. Arms are not given to Englishwomen either to fight the enemy or to defend herself. She must lie weaponless tonight. Yet if she believes that the fight going on up in the sky is a fight by the English to protect freedom, by the Germans to destroy freedom, she must fight, so far as she can, on the side of the English. How far can she fight for freedom without firearms? By making arms, or clothes or food. But there is another way of fighting for freedom without arms; we can fight with the mind. We can make ideas that will help the young Englishman who is fighting up in the sky to defeat the enemy.

But to make ideas effective, we must be able to fire them off. We must put them into action. And the hornet in the sky rouses another hornet in the mind. There was one zooming in *The Times* this morning—a woman's voice saying, "Women have not a word to say in politics." There is no woman in the Cabinet; nor in any responsible post. All the idea makers who are in a position to make ideas effective are men. That is a thought that damps thinking, and encourages irresponsibility. Why not bury the head in the pillow, plug the ears, and cease this futile activity of idea making? Because there are other tables besides officer tables and conference tables. Are we not leaving the young Englishman without a weapon that might be of value to him if we give up private thinking, tea-table thinking, because it seems useless? Are we not stressing our disability because our ability exposes us perhaps to abuse, perhaps to contempt? "I will not cease from mental fight," Blake wrote. Mental fight means thinking against the current, not with it.

That current flows fast and furious. It issues in a spate of words from the loudspeakers and the politicians. Every day they tell us that we are a free people, fighting to defend freedom. That is the current that has whirled the young airman up into the sky and keeps him circling there among the clouds. Down here, with a roof to cover us and a gas mask handy, it is our business to puncture gas bags and discover seeds of truth. It is not true that we are free. We are both prisoners tonight—he boxed up in his machine with a gun handy; we lying in the dark with a gas mask handy. If we were free we should be out in the open, dancing, at the play, or sitting at the window talking together. What is it that prevents us? "Hitler!" the loudspeakers cry with one voice. Who is Hitler? What is he? Aggressiveness, tyranny, the insane love of power made manifest, they reply. Destroy that, and you will be free.

The drone of the planes is now like the sawing of a branch overhead. Round and round it goes, sawing and sawing at a branch directly above the house. Another sound begins sawing its way in the brain. "Women of ability"—it was Lady Astor speaking in *The Times* this morning—"are held down because of a subconscious Hitlerism in the hearts of men." Certainly we are held down. We are equally prisoners tonight—the Englishmen in their planes, the Englishwomen in their beds. But if he stops to think he may be killed; and we too. So let us think for him. Let us try to drag up into consciousness the subconscious Hitlerism that holds us down. It is the desire for aggression; the desire to dominate and enslave. Even in the darkness we can see that made visible. We can see shop windows blazing; and women gazing; painted women; dressed-up women; women with crimson lips and crimson finger-nails. They are slaves who are trying to enslave. If we could free ourselves from slavery we should free men from tyranny. Hitlers are bred by slaves.

A bomb drops. All the windows rattle. The anti-aircraft guns are getting active. Up there on the hill under a net tagged with strips of green and brown stuff to imitate the hues of autumn leaves guns are concealed. Now they all fire at once. On the nine o'clock radio we shall be told "Forty-four enemy planes were shot down during the night, ten of them by anti-aircraft fire." And one of the terms of peace, the loudspeakers say, is to be disarmament. There are to be no more guns, no army, no navy, no air force in the future. No more young men will be trained to fight with arms. That rouses another mind-hornet in the chambers of the brain—another quotation. "To fight against a real enemy, to earn undying honour and glory by shooting total strangers, and to come home with my breast covered with medals and decorations, that was the summit of my hope . . . It was for this that my whole life so far had been dedicated, my education, training, everything . . ."

Those were the words of a young Englishman who fought in the last war. In the face of them, do the current thinkers honestly believe that by writing "Disarmament" on a sheet of paper at a conference table they will have done all that is needful? Othello's occupation will be gone;

but he will remain Othello. The young airman up in the sky is driven not only by the voices of loudspeakers; he is driven by voices in himself— ancient instincts, instincts fostered and cherished by education and tradition. Is he to be blamed for those instincts? Could we switch off the maternal instinct at the command of a table full of politicians? Suppose that imperative among the peace terms was: "Childbearing is to be restricted to a very small class of specially selected women," would we submit? Should we not say, "The maternal instinct is a woman's glory. It was for this that my whole life has been dedicated, my education, training, everything." . . . But if it were necessary, for the sake of humanity, for the peace of the world, that childbearing should be restricted, the maternal instinct subdued, women would attempt it. Men would help them. They would honour them for their refusal to bear children. They would give them other openings for their creative power. That too must make part of our fight for freedom. We must help the young Englishmen to root out from themselves the love of medals and decorations. We must create more honourable activities for those who try to conquer in themselves their fighting instinct, their subconscious Hitlerism. We must compensate the man for the loss of his gun.

The sound of sawing overhead has increased. All the searchlights are erect. They point at a spot exactly above this roof. At any moment a bomb may fall on this very room. One, two, three, four, five, six . . . the seconds pass. The bomb did not fall. But during those seconds of suspense all thinking stopped. All feeling, save one dull dread, ceased. A nail fixed the whole being to one hard board. The emotion of fear and of hate is therefore sterile, unfertile. Directly that fear passes, the mind reaches out and instinctively revives itself by trying to create. Since the room is dark it can create only from memory. It reaches out to the memory of other Augusts—in Bayreuth, listening to Wagner; in Rome, walking over the Campagna; in London. Friends' voices come back. Scraps of poetry return. Each of those thoughts, even in memory, was far more positive, reviving, healing and creative than the dull dread made of fear and hate. Therefore if we are to compensate the young man for the loss of his glory and of his gun, we must give him access to the creative feelings. We must make happiness. We must free him from the machine. We must bring him out of his prison into the open air. But what is the use of freeing the young Englishman if the young German and the young Italian remain slaves?

The searchlights, wavering across the flat, have picked up the plane now. From this window one can see a little silver insect turning and twisting in the light. The guns go pop pop pop. Then they cease. Probably the raider was brought down behind the hill. One of the pilots landed safe in a field near here the other day. He said to his captors, speaking fairly good English, "How glad I am that the fight is over!" Then an Englishman gave him a cigarette, and an Englishwoman made him a cup of tea. That would seem to show that if you can free the man from the machine, the seed does not fall upon altogether stony ground. The seed may be fertile.

At last all the guns have stopped firing. All the searchlights have been extinguished. The natural darkness of a summer's night returns. The innocent sounds of the country are heard again. An apple thuds to the ground. An owl hoots, winging its way from tree to tree. And some half-forgotten words of an old English writer come to mind: "The huntsmen are up in America . . ." Let us send these fragmentary notes to the huntsmen who are up in America, to the men and women whose sleep has not yet been broken by machine-gun fire, in the belief that they will rethink them generously and charitably, perhaps shape them into something serviceable. And now, in the shadowed half of the world, to sleep.

*August 1940*

JAMES BOSWELL

**On War**

While viewing, as travellers usually do, the remarkable objects of curiosity at Venice, I was conducted through the different departments of the Arsenal; and as I contemplated that great storehouse of mortal engines, in which there is not only a large deposit of arms, but men are continually employed in making more, my thoughts *rebounded*, if I may use the expression, from what I beheld; and the effect was, that I was first as it were stunned into a state of amazement, and when I recovered from that, my mind expanded itself in reflections upon the horrid irrationality of war.

What those reflections were I do not precisely recollect. But the general impression dwells upon my memory; and however strange it may seem, my opinion of the irrationality of war is still associated with the Arsenal of Venice.

One particular however I well remember. When I saw workingmen engaged with grave assiduity in fashioning weapons of death, I was struck with wonder at the shortsightedness, the *caecae mentes* of human beings, who were thus soberly preparing the instruments of destruction of their own species. I have since found upon a closer study of man, that my wonder might have been spared; because there are very few men whose minds are sufficiently enlarged to comprehend universal or even extensive good. The views of most individuals are limited to their own happiness; and the workmen whom I beheld so busy in the Arsenal of Venice saw nothing but what was good in the labour for which they received such wages as procured them the comforts of life. That their immediate satisfaction was not hindered by a view of the remote consequential and contingent evils for which alone their labours could be at all useful, would not surprise one who has had a tolerable share of experience in life. We must have the telescope of philosophy to make us perceive distant ills; nay, we know that there are individuals of our species to whom the immediate misery of others is nothing in comparison with their own advantage—for we know that in every age there have been found men very willing to perform the office of executioner even for a moderate hire.

To prepare instruments for the destruction of our species at large, is what I now see may very well be done by ordinary men, without starting, when they themselves are to run no risk. But I shall never forget, nor cease to wonder at a most extraordinary instance of thoughtless intrepidity which I had related to me by a cousin of mine, now a lieutenant-colonel in the British army, who was upon guard when it happened. A soldier of one of the regiments in garrison at Minorca, having been found guilty of a capital crime, was brought out to be hanged. They had neglected to have a rope in readiness, and the shocking business was at a stand. The fellow, with a spirit and alertness which in a general would, upon a difficult and trying emergency, have been very great presence of mind and conduct, stript the lace off his hat, said this will do, and actually made it serve as the fatal cord.

The irrationality of war is, I suppose, admitted by almost all men: I say almost all; because I have myself met with men who attempted seriously to maintain that it is an agreeable occupation and one of the chief means of human happiness. I must own that although I use the plural number here, I should have used the dual, had I been writing in Greek; for I never met with but two men who supported such a paradox; and one of them was a tragick poet, and one a Scotch Highlander. The first had his imagination so much in a blaze with heroic sentiments, with the "pride, pomp and circumstance of glorious war," that he did not advert to its miseries, as one dazzled with the pageantry of a magnificent funeral thinks not of the pangs of dissolution and the dismal corpse. The second had his attention so eagerly fixed on the advantage which accrued to his *clan* from "the trade of war," that he could think of it only as a good.

We are told by some writers, who assume the character of philosophers, that war is necessary to take off the superfluity of the human species, or at least to rid the world of numbers of idle and profligate men who are a burthen upon every community, and would grow an insupportable burthen, were they to live as long as men do in the usual course of nature. But there is unquestionably no reason to fear a superfluity of mankind, when we know that although perhaps the time "when every rood of land maintain'd its man" is a poetical exaggeration, yet vigorous and well directed industry can raise sustenance for such a proportion of people in a certain space of territory, as is astonishing to us who are accustomed to see only moderate effects of labour; and when we also know what immense regions of the terrestrial globe in very good climates are uninhabited. In these there is room for millions to enjoy existence. In cultivating these, the idle and profligate, expelled from their original societies, might be employed and gradually reformed, which would be better surely, than continuing the practice of periodical destruction, which is also indiscriminate, and involves the best equally with the worst of men.

I have often thought that if war should cease over all the face of the earth, for a thousand years, its reality would not be believed at such a distance of time, notwithstanding the faith of authentick records in every nation. Were mankind totally free from every tincture of prejudice in favour of those gallant exertions which could not exist were there not the evil of violence to combat; had they never seen in their own days, or been told by their fathers or grandfathers, of battles, and were there no traces remaining of the *art of war*, I have no doubt that they would treat as fabulous or allegorical, the accounts in history, of prodigious armies being formed, of men who engaged themselves for an unlimited time, under the penalty of immediate death, to obey implicitly the orders of commanders to whom they were not attached either by affection or by interest; that those armies were sometimes led with toilsome expedition over vast tracts of land, sometimes crouded into ships, and obliged to endure tedious, unhealthy, and perilous voyages; and that the purpose of all this toil and danger was not to obtain any comfort or pleasure, but to be in a situation to encounter other armies; and that those opposite multitudes the individuals of which had no cause of quarrel, no ill-will to each other, continued for hours engaged with patient and obstinate perseverance, while thousands were slain, and thousands crushed and mangled by diversity of wounds.

We who have from our earliest years had our minds filled with scenes of war of which we have read in the books that we most revere and most admire, who have remarked it in every revolving century, and in every country that has been discovered by navigators, even in the gentle and benign regions of the southern oceans; we who have seen all the intelligence, power and ingenuity of our nation employed in war, who have been accustomed to peruse Gazettes, and have had our friends and relations killed or sent home to us wretchedly maimed; we cannot without a steady effort of reflection be sensible of the improbability that rational beings should act so irrationally as to unite in deliberate plans, which must certainly produce the direful effects which war is known to do. But I have no doubt that if the project for a perpetual peace which the *Abbé de St. Pierre* sketched, and *Rousseau* improved, were to take place, the incredibility of war would after the lapse of some ages be universal.

Were there any good produced by war which could in any degree compensate its direful effects; were better men to spring up from the ruins of those who fall in battle, as more beautiful material forms sometimes arise from the ashes of others; or were those who escape from its destruction to have an increase of happiness; in short, were there any great beneficial effect to follow it, the notion of its irrationality would be only the notion of narrow comprehension. But we find that war is followed by no general good whatever. The power, the glory, or the wealth of a very few may be enlarged. But the people in general, upon both sides, after all the sufferings are passed, pursue their ordinary occupations, with no difference from their former state. The evils therefore of war, upon a general view of humanity are as the French say, *à pure perte*, a mere loss without any advantage, unless indeed furnishing subjects for history, poetry, and painting. And although it should be allowed that mankind have gained enjoyment in these respects, I suppose it will not be seriously said, that the misery is overbalanced. At any rate, there is already such a store of subjects, that an addition to them would be dearly purchased by more wars.

I am none of those who would set up their notions against the opinion of the world; on the contrary, I have such a respect for that authority, as to doubt my own judgement when it opposes that of numbers probably as wise as I am. But when I maintain the irrationality of war, I am not contradicting the opinion, but the practice of the world. For, as I have already observed, its irrationality is generally admitted. *Horace calls Hannibal, demens*, a madman; and Pope gives the same appellation to Alexander the Great and Charles XII.

*"From Macedonia's madman to the Swede."*

How long war will continue to be practised, we have no means of conjecturing. Civilization, which it might have been expected would have abolished it, has only refined its savage rudeness. The irrationality remains, though we have learnt *insanire certa ratione modoque*, to have a method in our madness.

That amiable religion which "proclaims peace on earth," hath not as yet made war to cease. The furious passions of men, modified as they are by moral instruction, still operate with much force; and by a perpetual fallacy, even the conscientious in each contending nation think they may join in war, because they each believe they are repelling an aggressor. Were the mild and humane doctrine of those Christians, who are called *Quakers*, which *Mr. Jenyns* has lately embellished with his elegant pen, to prevail, human felicity would gain more than we can well conceive. But perhaps it is necessary that mankind in this state of existence, the purpose of which is so mysterious, should ever suffer the woes of war.

To relieve my readers from reflections which they may think too abstract, I shall conclude this paper with a few observations upon actual war. In ancient times when a battle was fought man to man, or as somebody has very well expressed it, was a group of duels, there was an opportunity for individuals to distinguish themselves by vigour and bravery. One who was a "*robustus acri militia,* hardy from keen warfare," could gratify his ambition for fame, by the exercise of his own personal qualities. It was therefore more reasonable then, for individuals to enlist, than it is in modern times; for, a battle now is truly nothing else than a huge conflict of opposite engines worked by men, who are themselves as machines directed by a few; and the event is not so frequently decided by what is intentionally done, as by accidents happening in the dreadful confusion. It is as if two towns in opposite territories should be set on fire at the same time, and victory should be declared to the inhabitants of that in which the flames were least destructive. We hear much of the conduct of generals; and *Addison* himself has represented the Duke of *Marlborough* directing an army in battle, as an "angel riding in a whirlwind and directing the storm." Nevertheless I much doubt if upon many occasions the immediate schemes of a commander have had certain effect; and I believe Sir *Callaghan O'Bralachan* in Mr. *Macklin's Love A la-mode* gives a very just account of modern battle: "There is so much doing every where that we cannot tell what is doing any where."

MARTIN LUTHER KING JR

**Nobel Lecture,
11 December 1964**

## The quest for peace and justice

It is impossible to begin this lecture without again expressing my deep appreciation to the Nobel Committee of the Norwegian Parliament for bestowing upon me and the civil rights movement in the United States such a great honor. Occasionally in life there are those moments of unutterable fulfillment which cannot be completely explained by those symbols called words. Their meaning can only be articulated by the inaudible language of the heart. Such is the moment I am presently experiencing. I experience this high and joyous moment not for myself alone but for those devotees of nonviolence who have moved so courageously against the ramparts of racial injustice and who in the process have acquired a new estimate of their own human worth. Many of them are young and cultured. Others are middle aged and middle class. The majority are poor and untutored. But they are all united in the quiet conviction that it is better to suffer in dignity than to accept segregation in humiliation. These are the real heroes of the freedom struggle: they are the noble people for whom I accept the Nobel Peace Prize.

This evening I would like to use this lofty and historic platform to discuss what appears to me to be the most pressing problem confronting mankind today. Modern man has brought this whole world to an awe-inspiring threshold of the future. He has reached new and astonishing peaks of scientific success. He has produced machines that think and instruments that peer into the unfathomable ranges of interstellar space. He has built gigantic bridges to span the seas and gargantuan buildings to kiss the skies. His airplanes and spaceships have dwarfed distance, placed time in chains, and carved highways through the stratosphere. This is a dazzling picture of modern man's scientific and technological progress.

Yet, in spite of these spectacular strides in science and technology, and still unlimited ones to come, something basic is missing. There is a sort of poverty of the spirit which stands in glaring contrast to our scientific and technological abundance. The richer we have become materially, the poorer we have become morally and spiritually. We have learned to fly the air like birds and swim the sea like fish, but we have not learned the simple art of living together as brothers.

Every man lives in two realms, the internal and the external. The internal is that realm of spiritual ends expressed in art, literature, morals, and religion. The external is that complex of devices, techniques, mechanisms, and instrumentalities by means of which we live. Our problem today is that we have allowed the internal to become lost in the external. We have allowed the means by which we live to outdistance the ends for which we live. So much of modern life can be summarized in that arresting dictum of the poet Thoreau: "Improved means to an unimproved end". This is the serious predicament, the deep and haunting problem confronting modern man. If we are to survive today, our moral and spiritual "lag" must be eliminated. Enlarged material powers spell enlarged peril if there is not proportionate growth of the soul. When the "without" of man's nature subjugates the "within", dark storm clouds begin to form in the world.

This problem of spiritual and moral lag, which

constitutes modern man's chief dilemma, expresses itself in three larger problems which grow out of man's ethical infantilism. Each of these problems, while appearing to be separate and isolated, is inextricably bound to the other. I refer to racial injustice, poverty, and war.

The first problem that I would like to mention is racial injustice. The struggle to eliminate the evil of racial injustice constitutes one of the major struggles of our time. The present upsurge of the Negro people of the United States grows out of a deep and passionate determination to make freedom and equality a reality "here" and "now". In one sense the civil rights movement in the United States is a special American phenomenon which must be understood in the light of American history and dealt with in terms of the American situation. But on another and more important level, what is happening in the United States today is a relatively small part of a world development.

We live in a day, says the philosopher Alfred North Whitehead, "when civilization is shifting its basic outlook: a major turning point in history where the presuppositions on which society is structured are being analyzed, sharply challenged, and profoundly changed." What we are seeing now is a freedom explosion, the realization of "an idea whose time has come", to use Victor Hugo's phrase. The deep rumbling of discontent that we hear today is the thunder of disinherited masses, rising from dungeons of oppression to the bright hills of freedom, in one majestic chorus the rising masses singing, in the words of our freedom song, "Ain't gonna let nobody turn us around." All over the world, like a fever, the freedom movement is spreading in the widest liberation in history. The great masses of people are determined to end the exploitation of their races and land. They are awake and moving toward their goal like a tidal wave. You can hear them rumbling in every village street, on the docks, in the houses, among the students, in the churches, and at political meetings. Historic movement was for several centuries that of the nations and societies of Western Europe out into the rest of the world in "conquest" of various sorts. That period, the era of colonialism, is at an end. East is meeting West. The earth is being redistributed. Yes, we are "shifting our basic outlooks".

These developments should not surprise any student of history. Oppressed people cannot remain oppressed forever. The yearning for freedom eventually manifests itself. The Bible tells the thrilling story of how Moses stood in Pharaoh's court centuries ago and cried, "Let my people go." This is a kind of opening chapter in a continuing story. The present struggle in the United States is a later chapter in the same unfolding story. Something within has reminded the Negro of his birthright of freedom, and something without has reminded him that it can be gained. Consciously or unconsciously, he has been caught up by the *Zeitgeist*, and with his black brothers of Africa and his brown and yellow brothers in Asia, South America, and the Caribbean, the United States Negro is moving with a sense of great urgency toward the promised land of racial justice.

Fortunately, some significant strides have been made in the struggle to end the long night of racial injustice. We have seen the magnificent drama of independence unfold in Asia and Africa. Just thirty years ago there were only three independent nations in the whole of Africa. But today thirty-five African nations have risen from colonial bondage. In the United States we have witnessed the gradual demise of the system of racial segregation. The Supreme Court's decision of 1954 outlawing segregation in the public schools gave a legal and constitutional deathblow to the whole doctrine of separate but equal. The Court decreed that separate facilities are inherently unequal and that to segregate a child on the basis of race is to deny that child equal protection of the law. This decision came as a beacon light of hope to millions of disinherited people. Then came that glowing day a few months ago when a strong Civil Rights Bill became the law of our land. This bill, which was first recommended and promoted by President Kennedy, was passed because of the overwhelming support and perseverance of millions of Americans, Negro and white. It came as a bright interlude in the long and sometimes turbulent struggle for civil rights: the beginning of a second emancipation proclamation providing a comprehensive legal basis for equality of opportunity. Since the passage of this bill we have seen some encouraging and surprising signs of compliance. I am happy to report that, by and large, communities all over the southern part of the United States are obeying the Civil Rights Law and showing remarkable good sense in the process.

Another indication that progress is being made was found in the recent presidential election in the United States. The American people revealed great maturity by overwhelmingly rejecting a presidential candidate who had become identified with extremism, racism, and retrogression. The voters of our nation rendered a telling blow to the radical right. They defeated those elements in our society which seek to pit white against Negro and lead the nation down a dangerous Fascist path.

Let me not leave you with a false impression. The problem is far from solved. We still have a long, long way to go before the dream of freedom is a reality for the Negro in the United States. To put it figuratively in biblical language, we have left the dusty soils of Egypt and crossed a Red Sea whose waters had for years been hardened by a long and piercing winter of massive resistance. But before we reach the majestic shores of the Promised Land, there is a frustrating and bewildering wilderness ahead. We must still face prodigious hilltops of opposition and gigantic mountains of resistance. But with patient and firm determination we will press on until every valley of despair is exalted to new peaks of hope, until every mountain of pride and irrationality is made low by the leveling process of humility and compassion; until the rough places of injustice are transformed into a smooth plane of equality of opportunity; and until the crooked places of prejudice are transformed by the straightening process of bright-eyed wisdom.

What the main sections of the civil rights movement in the United States are saying is that the demand for dignity, equality, jobs, and citizenship will not be abandoned or diluted or postponed. If that means resistance and conflict we shall not flinch. We shall not be cowed. We are no longer afraid.

The word that symbolizes the spirit and the outward form of our encounter is *nonviolence*, and it is doubtless that factor which made it seem appropriate to award a peace prize to one identified with struggle. Broadly speaking, nonviolence in the civil rights struggle has meant not relying on arms and weapons of struggle. It has meant noncooperation with customs and laws which are institutional aspects of a regime of discrimination and enslavement. It has meant direct participation of masses in protest, rather than reliance on indirect methods which frequently do not involve masses in action at all.

Nonviolence has also meant that my people in the agonizing struggles of recent years have taken suffering upon themselves instead of inflicting it on others. It has meant, as I said, that we are no longer afraid and cowed. But in some substantial degree it has meant that we do not want to instill fear in others or into the society of which we are a part. The movement does not seek to liberate Negroes at the expense of the humiliation and enslavement of whites. It seeks no victory over anyone. It seeks to liberate American society and to share in the self-liberation of all the people.

Violence as a way of achieving racial justice is both impractical and immoral. I am not unmindful of the fact that violence often brings about momentary results. Nations have frequently won their independence in battle. But in spite of temporary victories, violence never brings permanent peace. It solves no social problem: it merely creates new and more complicated ones. Violence is impractical because it is a descending spiral ending in destruction for all. It is immoral because it seeks to humiliate the opponent rather than win his understanding: it seeks to annihilate rather than convert. Violence is immoral because it thrives on hatred rather than love. It destroys community and makes brotherhood impossible. It leaves society in monologue rather than dialogue. Violence ends up defeating itself. It creates bitterness in the survivors and brutality in the destroyers.

In a real sense nonviolence seeks to redeem the spiritual and moral lag that I spoke of earlier as the chief dilemma of modern man. It seeks to secure moral ends through moral means. Nonviolence is a powerful and just weapon. Indeed, it is a weapon unique in history, which cuts without wounding and ennobles the man who wields it.

I believe in this method because I think it is the only way to reestablish a broken community. It is the method which seeks to implement the just law by appealing to the conscience of the great decent majority who through blindness, fear, pride, and irrationality have allowed their consciences to sleep.

The nonviolent resisters can summarize their message in the following simple terms: we will take direct action against injustice despite the failure of governmental and other official agencies to act first. We will not obey unjust laws or submit to unjust practices. We will do this peacefully, openly, cheerfully because our aim is to persuade. We adopt the means of nonviolence because our end is a community at peace with itself. We will try to persuade with our words, but if our words fail, we will try to persuade with our acts. We will always be willing to talk and seek fair compromise, but we are ready to suffer when

necessary and even risk our lives to become witnesses to truth as we see it.

This approach to the problem of racial injustice
is not at all without successful precedent. It was
used in a magnificent way by Mohandas K. Gandhi
to challenge the might of the British Empire and
free his people from the political domination and
economic exploitation inflicted upon them for
centuries. He struggled only with the weapons of
truth, soul force, non-injury, and courage.

In the past ten years unarmed gallant men and
women of the United States have given living
testimony to the moral power and efficacy of nonviolence. By the thousands, faceless, anonymous,
relentless young people, black and white, have
temporarily left the ivory towers of learning for
the barricades of bias. Their courageous and dis-
ciplined activities have come as a refreshing oasis
in a desert sweltering with the heat of injustice.
They have taken our whole nation back to those
great wells of democracy which were dug deep
by the founding fathers in the formulation of the
Constitution and the Declaration of Independence. One day all of America will be proud of
their achievements.

I am only too well aware of the human weak-
nesses and failures which exist, the doubts about

the efficacy of nonviolence, and the open advocacy of violence by some. But I am still convinced that nonviolence is both the most practically sound and morally excellent way to grapple with the age-old problem of racial injustice.

A second evil which plagues the modern world is that of poverty. Like a monstrous octopus, it projects its nagging, prehensile tentacles in lands and villages all over the world. Almost two-thirds of the peoples of the world go to bed hungry at night.

They are undernourished, ill-housed, and shabbily clad. Many of them have no houses or beds to sleep in. Their only beds are the sidewalks of the cities and the dusty roads of the villages. Most of these poverty-stricken children of God have never seen a physician or a dentist. This problem of poverty is not only seen in the class division between the highly developed industrial nations and the so-called underdeveloped nations; it is seen in the great economic gaps within the rich nations themselves. Take my own country for example. We have developed the greatest system of production that history has ever known. We have become the richest nation in the world. Our national gross product this year will reach the astounding figure of almost 650 billion dollars.

Yet, at least one-fifth of our fellow citizens – some ten million families, comprising about forty million individuals – are bound to a miserable culture of poverty. In a sense the poverty of the poor in America is more frustrating than the poverty of Africa and Asia. The misery of the poor in Africa and Asia is shared misery, a fact of life for the vast majority; they are all poor together as a result of years of exploitation and underdevelopment. In sad contrast, the poor in America know that they live in the richest nation in the world, and that even though they are perishing on a lonely island of poverty they are surrounded by a vast ocean of material prosperity. Glistening towers of glass and steel easily seen from their slum dwellings spring up almost overnight. Jet liners speed over their ghettoes at 600 miles an hour; satellites streak through outer space and reveal details of the moon. President Johnson, in his State of the Union Message, emphasized this contradiction when he heralded the United States' "highest standard of living in the world", and deplored that it was accompanied by "dislocation; loss of jobs, and the specter of poverty in the midst of plenty".

So it is obvious that if man is to redeem his spiritual and moral "lag", he must go all out to bridge the social and economic gulf between the "haves" and the "have nots" of the world. Poverty is one of the most urgent items on the agenda of modern life.

There is nothing new about poverty. What is new, however, is that we have the resources to get rid of it. More than a century and a half ago people began to be disturbed about the twin problems of population and production. A thoughtful Englishman named Malthus wrote a book that set forth some rather frightening conclusions. He predicted that the human family was gradually moving toward global starvation because the world was producing people faster than it was producing food and material to support them. Later scientists, however, disproved the conclusion of Malthus, and revealed that he had vastly underestimated the resources of the world and the resourcefulness of man.

Not too many years ago, Dr. Kirtley Mather, a Harvard geologist, wrote a book entitled *Enough and to Spare*. He set forth the basic theme that famine is wholly unnecessary in the modern world. Today, therefore, the question on the agenda must read: Why should there be hunger and privation in any land, in any city, at any table when man has the resources and the scientific know-how to provide all mankind with the basic necessities of life? Even deserts can be irrigated and top soil can be replaced. We cannot complain of a lack of land, for there are twenty-five million square miles of tillable land, of which we are using less than seven million. We have amazing knowledge of vitamins, nutrition, the chemistry of food, and the versatility of atoms. There is no deficit in human resources; the deficit is in human will. The well-off and the secure have too often become indifferent and oblivious to the poverty and deprivation in their midst. The poor in our countries have been shut out of our minds, and driven from the mainstream of our societies, because we have allowed them to become invisible. Just as nonviolence exposed the ugliness of racial injustice, so must the infection and sickness of poverty be exposed and healed – not only its symptoms but its basic causes. This, too, will be a fierce struggle, but we must not be afraid to pursue the remedy no matter how formidable the task.

The time has come for an all-out world war against poverty. The rich nations must use their vast resources of wealth to develop the underdeveloped, school the unschooled, and feed the unfed. Ultimately a great nation is a compassionate nation. No individual or nation can be great if it does not have a concern for "the least of these". Deeply etched in the fiber of our religious tradition is the conviction that men are made in the image of God and that they are souls of infinite metaphysical value, the heirs of a legacy of dignity and worth. If we feel this as a profound moral fact, we cannot be content to see men hungry, to see men victimized with starvation and ill health when we have the means to help them. The wealthy nations must go all out to bridge the gulf between the rich minority and the poor majority.

In the final analysis, the rich must not ignore the poor because both rich and poor are tied in a single garment of destiny. All life is interrelated, and all men are interdependent. The agony of the poor diminishes the rich, and the salvation of the poor enlarges the rich. We are inevitably our brothers' keeper because of the interrelated structure of reality. John Donne interpreted this truth in graphic terms when he affirmed:

> No man is an Iland, intire of its selfe: every
> man is a peece of the Continent, a part of the
> maine: if a Clod bee washed away by the Sea,
> Europe is the lesse, as well as if a Promontorie

*were, as well as if a Mannor of thy friends*
*or of thine owne were: any mans death*
*diminishes me, because I am involved in*
*Mankinde: and therefore never send to know*
*for whom the bell tolls: it tolls for thee.*

A third great evil confronting our world is that
of war. Recent events have vividly reminded us that
nations are not reducing but rather increasing
their arsenals of weapons of mass destruction.
The best brains in the highly developed nations of
the world are devoted to military technology. The
proliferation of nuclear weapons has not been
halted, in spite of the Limited Test Ban Treaty.
On the contrary, the detonation of an atomic
device by the first non-white, non-Western, and
so-called underdeveloped power, namely the
Chinese People's Republic, opens new vistas
of exposure of vast multitudes, the whole of
humanity, to insidious terrorization by the ever-
present threat of annihilation. The fact that most
of the time human beings put the truth about
the nature and risks of the nuclear war out of
their minds because it is too painful and therefore not "acceptable", does not alter the nature
and risks of such war. The device of "rejection"

may temporarily cover up anxiety, but it does not bestow peace of mind and emotional security.

So man's proneness to engage in war is still a fact. But wisdom born of experience should tell us that war is obsolete. There may have been a time when war served as a negative good by preventing the spread and growth of an evil force, but the destructive power of modern weapons eliminated even the possibility that war may serve as a negative good. If we assume that life is worth living and that man has a right to survive, then we must find an alternative to war. In a day when vehicles hurtle through outer space and guided ballistic missiles carve highways of death through the stratosphere, no nation can claim victory in war. A so-called limited war will leave little more than a calamitous legacy of human suffering, political turmoil, and spiritual disillusionment. A world war – God forbid! – will leave only smoldering ashes as a mute testimony of a human race whose folly led inexorably to ultimate death. So if modern man continues to flirt unhesitatingly with war, he will transform his earthly habitat into an inferno such as even the mind of Dante could not imagine.

Therefore, I venture to suggest to all of you and all who hear and may eventually read these words, that the philosophy and strategy of non-violence become immediately a subject for study and for serious experimentation in every field of human conflict, by no means excluding the relations between nations. It is, after all, nation-states which make war, which have produced the weapons which threaten the survival of mankind, and which are both genocidal and suicidal in character.

Here also we have ancient habits to deal with, vast structures of power, indescribably complicated problems to solve. But unless we abdicate our humanity altogether and succumb to fear and impotence in the presence of the weapons we have ourselves created, it is as imperative and urgent to put an end to war and violence between nations as it is to put an end to racial injustice. Equality with whites will hardly solve the problems of either whites or Negroes if it means equality in a society under the spell of terror and a world doomed to extinction.

I do not wish to minimize the complexity of the problems that need to be faced in achieving disarmament and peace. But I think it is a fact that we shall not have the will, the courage, and the insight to deal with such matters unless in this field we are prepared to undergo a mental and spiritual reevaluation – a change of focus which will enable us to see that the things which seem most real and powerful are indeed now unreal and have come under the sentence of death. We need to make a supreme effort to generate the readiness, indeed the eagerness, to enter into the new world which is now possible, "the city which hath foundations, whose builder and maker is God".

We will not build a peaceful world by following a negative path. It is not enough to say "We must not wage war." It is necessary to love peace and sacrifice for it. We must concentrate not merely on the negative expulsion of war, but on the positive affirmation of peace. There is a fascinating little story that is preserved for us in Greek literature about Ulysses and the Sirens. The Sirens had the ability to sing so sweetly that sailors could not resist steering toward their island. Many ships were lured upon the rocks, and men forgot home, duty, and honor as they flung themselves into the sea to be embraced by arms that drew them down to death. Ulysses, determined not to be lured by the Sirens, first decided to tie himself tightly to the mast of his boat, and his crew stuffed their ears with wax. But finally he and his crew learned a better way to save themselves:

they took on board the beautiful singer Orpheus whose melodies were sweeter than the music of the Sirens. When Orpheus sang, who bothered to listen to the Sirens?

So we must fix our vision not merely on the negative expulsion of war, but upon the positive affirmation of peace. We must see that peace represents a sweeter music, a cosmic melody that is far superior to the discords of war. Somehow we must transform the dynamics of the world power struggle from the negative nuclear arms race which no one can win to a positive contest to harness man's creative genius for the purpose of making peace and prosperity a reality for all of the nations of the world. In short, we must shift the arms race into a "peace race". If we have the will and determination to mount such a peace offensive, we will unlock hitherto tightly sealed doors of hope and transform our imminent cosmic elegy into a psalm of creative fulfillment.

All that I have said boils down to the point of affirming that mankind's survival is dependent upon man's ability to solve the problems of racial injustice, poverty, and war; the solution of these problems is in turn dependent upon man squaring his moral progress with his scientific progress, and learning the practical art of living in harmony. Some years ago a famous novelist died. Among his papers was found a list of suggested story plots for future stories, the most prominently underscored being this one: "A widely separated family inherits a house in which they have to live together." This is the great new problem of mankind. We have inherited a big house, a great "world house" in which we have to live together – black and white, Easterners and Westerners, Gentiles and Jews, Catholics and Protestants, Moslem and Hindu, a family unduly separated in ideas, culture, and interests who, because we can never again live without each other, must learn, somehow, in this one big world, to live with each other.

This means that more and more our loyalties must become ecumenical rather than sectional. We must now give an overriding loyalty to mankind as a whole in order to preserve the best in our individual societies.

This call for a worldwide fellowship that lifts neighborly concern beyond one's tribe, race, class, and nation is in reality a call for an all-embracing and unconditional love for all men. This oft misunderstood and misinterpreted concept so readily dismissed by the Nietzsches of the world as a weak and cowardly force, has now become an absolute necessity for the survival of man. When I speak of love I am not speaking of some sentimental and weak response which is little more than emotional bosh. I am speaking of that force which all of the great religions have seen as the supreme unifying principle of life. Love is somehow the key that unlocks the door which leads to ultimate reality. This Hindu-Moslem-Christian-Jewish-Buddhist belief about ultimate reality is beautifully summed up in the First Epistle of Saint John:

> Let us love one another: for love is of God; and everyone that loveth is born of God, and knoweth God.
> He that loveth not knoweth not God; for God is love.
> If we love one another, God dwelleth in us, and His love is perfected in us.

Let us hope that this spirit will become the order of the day. As Arnold Toynbee says: "Love is the ultimate force that makes for the saving choice of life and good against the damning choice of death and evil. Therefore the first hope in our inventory must be the hope that love is going to have the last word." We can no longer afford to worship the God of hate or bow before the altar of retaliation. The oceans of history are made turbulent by the ever-rising tides of hate. History is cluttered with the wreckage of nations and individuals that pursued this selfdefeating path of hate. Love is the key to the solution of the problems of the world.

Let me close by saying that I have the personal faith that mankind will somehow rise up to the occasion and give new directions to an age drifting rapidly to its doom. In spite of the tensions and uncertainties of this period something profoundly meaningful is taking place. Old systems of exploitation and oppression are passing away, and out of the womb of a frail world new systems of justice and equality are being born. Doors of opportunity are gradually being opened to those at the bottom of society. The shirtless and barefoot people of the land are developing a new sense of "some-bodiness" and carving a tunnel of hope through the dark mountain of despair. "The people who sat in darkness have seen a great light." Here and there an individual or group dares to love, and rises to the majestic heights of moral maturity. So in a real sense this is a great time to be alive. Therefore, I am not yet discouraged about the future. Granted that the easygoing optimism of yesterday is impossible. Granted that those who pioneer in the struggle for peace and freedom will still face uncomfortable jail terms, painful threats of death; they will still be battered by the storms of persecution, leading them to the nagging feeling that they can no longer bear such a heavy burden, and the temptation of wanting to retreat to a more quiet and serene life. Granted that we face a world crisis which leaves us standing so often amid the surging murmur of life's restless sea. But every crisis has both its dangers and its opportunities. It can spell either salvation or doom. In a dark confused world the kingdom of God may yet reign in the hearts of men.

# Permissions Acknowledgements

'Bed' by Rose Macaulay reproduced by permission of The Society of Authors as the Literary Representative of the Estate of Rose Macaulay.

'Nobel Lecture, 11 December 1964' by Martin Luther King Jr reprinted by arrangement with The Heirs to the Estate of Martin Luther King Jr, c/o Writers House as agent for the proprietor New York, NY.

'Bed-books and Night-lights' by H. M. Tomlinson reprinted by permission of Peters Fraser & Dunlop (www.petersfraserdunlop.com) on behalf of the Estate of H. M. Tomlinson.

'Thoughts on Peace in an Air Raid' by Virginia Woolf reproduced by permission of The Society of Authors as the Literary Representative of the Estate of Virginia Woolf.

'Thoughts on Peace in an Air Raid' from *The Death of The Moth and Other Essays* by Virginia Woolf. Copyright © 1942 by Harcourt Brace Jovanovich, Inc. Copyright © 1970 by Marjorie T. Parsons, Executrix. Used by permission of HarperCollins Publishers.